�֍ The Pagoda and The Cross

The
PAGODA
and
The CROSS

THE LIFE OF BISHOP FORD OF MARYKNOLL

❁

JOHN F. DONOVAN, M.M.

❁

CHARLES SCRIBNER'S SONS
New York

B
F

FOREWORD

Bishop Francis Xavier Ford, M.M. was in America on furlough from China when I first met him in 1929 shortly after I came to Maryknoll from Holy Cross College. At the time of his episcopal consecration at Maryknoll in 1935, I told the new bishop that it was my deep desire to go to China, and, if possible, to his Kaying mission. Although he seemed to be joking when he promised to see what he could do with our Maryknoll superiors, three years later I was assigned to the Kaying Vicariate.

When the Japanese captured Canton in November 1938, I was in Hong Kong, where Bishop Ford had sent me to do emergency relief work among the refugees fleeing into the British colony. In June 1939, he assigned me to the pro-cathedral parish in Kaying City as assistant. A year later I was appointed pastor of this parish. From 1939 to 1943, I lived in a rented Chinese house with Bishop Ford; and after 1943, when he took over the directorship of a students' hostel two hundred yards away, we lived as neighbors until the advance of the Communists and my return to the United States.

It seems presumptuous of me, neither biographer nor missiologist, to attempt the story of Maryknoll's great pioneer missioner. My only qualifications are my long association with Bishop Ford and my deep admiration for him. The following pages may serve to keep his memory fresh until someone undertakes the definitive biography.

JOHN F. DONOVAN, M.M.

Maryknoll, New York
January 1967

CONTENTS

viii

PROLOGUE

Bishop Ford's tribulations among the Chinese people and his arrest and death at the hands of the Communists can be understood only in terms of the history of China's experiences with the Christian West. Years of oppression, brutality, and exploitation had engendered among the Chinese a feeling of distrust and animosity toward all foreigners. Western, wealthy, warlike—that was the image of the foreigner. Colonialism, capitalism, Christianity—a triple threat inextricably intertwined. The Oriental's distrust of Western civilization developed gradually, more than a thousand years in the making.

In the year 635 Christianity was introduced into China from Syria by Nestorian Christians—an heretical sect condemned in the year 431 by the Council of Ephesus. They were hospitably received, particularly by the T'ang monarchs, and for almost two hundred years they were permitted to preach Christianity and accept converts. Their mission method was quite simple. They set up monasteries and translated the Christian message into Chinese, using Confucian, Buddhist, and Taoist idiom more successfully perhaps than succeeding missioners. However, with the collapse of the T'ang dynasty at the beginning of the tenth century, a series of persecutions drove the Nestorian missioners and many of their followers from the empire. One weakness in their mission effort was their failure to train native Christian leaders, priests or laymen. In 1264 when Marco Polo began his seventeen years of travel throughout China, he found isolated remnants of Nestorian Christianity.

The *Book of Marco Polo*, with its stories of China's wealth and vastness, its mighty rivers and huge cities, its bridges and beautiful palaces, had a tremendous impact on thirteenth- and fourteenth-century Europe. Merchants recognized the possibility for enormous profits in the fabulous accounts of Chinese silk, ivory carvings, tea, printing presses, and gunpowder.

The Church saw a vast pagan world awaiting the gospel. The Yüan emperor gave Marco Polo a message for the Pope requesting one hundred men "wise in the Christian law and acquainted with the seven arts." He promised the special patronage of the imperial throne. Unfortunately little was done to take advantage of the extraordinary opportunity. The Italian Franciscan, John of Montecorvino, reached Peking in 1292 and throughout the fourteenth century several small groups of Franciscans arrived in China. With money from Europe they built churches and friaries. One of the churches, built in 1366, called the Temple of the Cross, was discovered in 1932. Its principal object of veneration was a cross of Maltese design on which were cut Chinese characters saying, "Look towards it [the Cross] and hope in it."

The Franciscans made some converts and a few Nestorian Christians were found and brought into the Church; however, the impact of the mission was of a minor nature. When the Ming dynasty replaced the Yüan regime, the patronage was withdrawn; Christians were persecuted, churches were destroyed, and the mission effort literally wiped out, for there was no trace of it when the Jesuit Fathers arrived two hundred years later.

Apart from the fact that the journey from Europe was long and hazardous, there were other reasons for the failure of the heroic Franciscan effort. There was no unified approach to the task of Christianizing the country. Many of the missioners did not have a thorough grasp of the Chinese language, and the Church was regarded by the people as a "foreign" institution, for—like the Nestorians—the Franciscans made no attempt to train native priests or lay leaders. It was not the practice at that time to do so.

After the Reformation, the Catholic Church seemed determined to compensate for the losses suffered in Europe by a renewed and intensified foreign mission effort. When the Spanish occupied the Philippines in 1565, they found many Chinese there. Encouraged by the success of their work among the uneducated Filipinos, the Spanish Dominicans, Franciscans, and Augustinians decided to evangelize the mainland of China. A small group landed at Canton in 1579—the leader "took possession of China in the name of Christ." The missioners walked through the streets determinedly holding aloft the Cross. Some were open in their criticism of Buddhist and other non-Christian religious practices and forbade converts to take part in any ceremony before the image or tablets of Confucius. But the Portuguese, jealous of their trade monopoly, incited the Chinese to expel the Spanish missioners. Rivalry between the nations carried over into rivalry between the religious orders.

At that time, the Church had a new foreign mission army in the recently established Society of Jesus. In their training, in their tact, in their motivation, the Jesuits were superb. And China, with its teeming millions of "souls to be saved from paganism," was the natural target for

Jesuit zeal and devotion. If China could be won, they said, it would more than compensate for the defections in Europe.

Because in the mid-sixteenth century missioners were excluded from China, St. Francis Xavier, the famous Jesuit "apostle to the Indies," was forced to by-pass China and to travel on to Japan. While there he discovered that much of Japan's culture and literature seemed to have originated in China and he decided to make another effort to enter the closed country. It was while he was preparing his approach that he died, in 1552, on Southeast China's offshore island of Sancian. A few decades later other members of the Society of Jesus were more successful in reaching the mainland.

The most famous and perhaps the most learned of the early Jesuits in China was Father Matteo Ricci. He had not resided in the country long when he appreciated the fact that he was encountering one of the most advanced societies then known. He recognized that it would not be enough merely to preach the gospel: he had to establish for the Christian religion some aspects of superiority before he could compete with religions of great antiquity and with cults deeply rooted in the Chinese nature. In 1582, on reaching Macao, the Portuguese enclave on the South China coast, Ricci plunged into the study of the Chinese language, literature, and philosophy. For nine years the missioner assiduously prepared himself. When he arrived in Peking, he astonished officials with his knowledge of Chinese culture and his perfect command of their difficult language.

Father Ricci and his companions, adopting the dress of the Chinese literati, concentrated their efforts on Peking's high officials. Relying on the power of charity, not on the force of arms, appealing to the intellect, not to the emotions, they won acceptance by the Chinese. Soon they had a number of converts to Christianity despite the strong cultural resistance.

Ricci was a skilled mathematician and astronomer, and he became an adviser on science and technology to the imperial court. Before long the Jesuits were revising the inaccurate Chinese calendar, preparing maps, and translating technological works into Chinese. They even consented to assist in the manufacture of military weapons. Ricci insisted that all Chinese military officers learn geometry and the Emperor gave him the responsibility for teaching it. "A wise, brave general should first learn geometry," said Ricci, "otherwise his wisdom and bravery would be exercised in vain." Because of their scientific contribution to the country, the Jesuits were granted *carte blanche* permission to preach the Christian religion.

The pioneer Jesuit missioners realized that they must present their message in terms the Chinese people could appropriate and they translated parts of the Roman missal and the doctrine into literary Chinese. But many who followed Ricci had neither his skill in language nor his tact. Five years after his death in 1610, Pope Paul V in accordance with the wish of the Jesuit St. Robert Bellarmine, had granted missioners in China the right to use literary Chinese in place of Latin in the liturgy. But the concession was not put into use. Despite their scholarship and apostolic zeal, the missioners preferred the Latin formula. Nor was this the only point at which they refused to compromise. As a matter of principle, the Catholic missioners could recognize no belief other than their own. This attitude put them at a decided disadvantage in discussing religion with Chinese intellectuals who held that no religion had a monopoly on the truth. The propensity of some priests to condemn other religions aroused the deep resentment and antagonism of many Chinese scholars and officials. The Jesuits did, however, succeed in preparing a number of minor officials for baptism, and during the anti-foreign persecutions of 1615 and 1621, they were given special protection in the Imperial city of Peking.

In the year 1622, Pope Gregory XV in his papal document *Inscrutabili Divinae* set up the Congregation for the Propagation of the Faith (*Congregatio de Propaganda Fide*) to give special emphasis to the eternal duty to preach the gospel to every nation; and to return to Rome the responsibility for the conversion of the non-Christian world, which for over a century had been exercised by the kings of Spain and Portugal. Thirty-seven years later the Congregation addressed a document to vicars apostolic leaving Europe for Tonkin and Cochin China. It stated that the missioners must understand the people to whom they preach the gospel, and pointed out the need to train a native clergy so that the mission country may become self-sufficient and self-propagating. This instruction in many instances and for many different reasons was not carried out. The deep prejudice against anything non-Western was perhaps the dominating factor, despite Propaganda's insistence that "the success of the mission does not lie in the perpetuating of the mission as such, but the substitution of a native clergy for the missionary clergy and eventually (the establishment of) a native hierarchy."

"Do not devote any zeal," the missioners were told in the 1659 document, "do not advance any argument to convince these people that they should change their rituals, their customs or their manners, unless these are obviously contrary to religion and morality. What could be more absurd than carrying France, Spain, Italy or any other European country to the Chinese? Do not introduce them to our countries, but to our faith."

What profound wisdom! Clearly the Church's position was one of supra-nationalism. In principle at least it did not identify itself with any colonial power or any one country's colonial designs although this could not be said of individual missioners, many of whom took advantage of their native country's political and military power to gain privileges in China.

Having a clear understanding of Chinese culture and traditions, the majority of the Jesuit missioners decided that if Christianity was to make any substantial headway in China, the Church must make concessions in favor of certain ancient Chinese customs, particularly the special national ceremonies honoring Confucius, and certain features of ancestor ritual. Ricci had attempted to interpret the Confucian texts in a manner favorable to the Christian doctrine, wisely contending that there were many parallels between Christ's teaching and the words of Confucius. Furthermore, Ricci had perceived that the Chinese regarded Confucius not as a god, but as a revered sage worthy of national homage, a philosopher whose notion of a Supreme Being was not incompatible with the Christian idea of God. But Ricci's attempt to establish a reciprocal understanding between East and West failed. To the detriment of the apostolic effort in China, Dominican and Franciscan missioners, along with a few Jesuits, disagreed with Ricci's view. They saw a conflict with Christian doctrine in all aspects of the ancestor ceremonial and in all rites honoring Confucius. They adamantly held that these Chinese practices were superstitious and had to be condemned.

History refers to this dispute as the "Chinese rites controversy." Ultimately the case was brought for a decision to Rome by the Dominican missioner, Father Juan Baptista Morales. In 1704, Pope Clement XI decreed that the Chinese Christians, "until it is decided otherwise," should be forbidden to take part in any ceremonies honoring Confucius or their ancestors. The papal legate sent to China to deliver the decision bungled the case still further by making a poor impression on proud Emperor K'ang-hsi. After reading the papal document, K'ang-hsi observed bitterly that the Westerners were rather narrow and that their religion was no different from the bigoted sects of Buddhism. He concluded by forbidding the preaching and practice of Christianity in China, "so there will be no more trouble."

Thus in a country that had built its civilization around the family and the concept of filial piety, and that honored scholarship and intellectual competence so highly, the intelligentsia disassociated itself from Christian thought and teaching. Because of the papal decree, any future Chinese convert to Christianity would have to forego all hope of official life; he would be considered a disgrace to his family, since he could no longer give honor to his ancestors; he would be disloyal to his country, since he could no longer pay homage to her greatest sage, the teacher of teachers, the molder of her intellectual and moral life. Cut off from his family, many a Chinese Christian would henceforth be ostracized by his village. The Church became a stumbling block to the potential Chinese convert. (Not until 1939 did Rome reverse its judgment regarding the Chinese rites. By then Pius XII's decision came too late.)

Despite the fact that the propagation and practice of Christianity were forbidden by the Chinese government, isolated and heroic missionary efforts continued. The eighteenth century and the early part of the nineteenth were decades of persecution, years of overpowering sadness for the Christian Church in China. Few records were kept, few memoirs were written. What we do know is that a sufficient number of European priests, at the risk of their lives, managed to enter China to keep alive the faith and to hold together what remained of the Church until the mid-nineteenth century treaties between China and the European powers guaranteed them protection.

Appraising the work of the Catholic missioners in China, from the "Jesuit period" to the arrival of the Western nations, we find much that was individually outstanding, much that was individually successful, notwithstanding the unsettled political conditions. But again there was no co-ordinated effort—there were in fact many bitter quarrels between various missionary groups. Each missioner was left to himself. When he was driven into exile or when he died, there was no assurance of continuity in his work. There was no attempt to train a Chinese secular clergy, although the Congregation of Propaganda, as early as 1630, urged the missioners to discover "the most intelligent among the Christians" and to "raise them to Holy Orders, up to and including the priesthood." The few Chinese young men who became priests belonged to religious Orders whose superiors were located outside the country. According to available correspondence, most European missioners apparently believed that the Chinese character was too weak to embrace the responsibility of the priesthood and so they did not encourage vocations.

At the halfway point of the nineteenth century, China was forced to give protection to European missioners and to Chinese Christians. At this time, converts to the Church, mostly the uneducated and the poor, increased substantially. In Europe, new mission-sending societies were founded. Communities of missionary Sisters, such as the Charity Sisters of St. Vincent de Paul and the Sisters of St. Paul of Chartres, began their labor of love for China's poor and for abandoned babies. Before the end of the century, Aurora

University was founded in Shanghai by the Jesuit Fathers, and Fu-jen University was opened in Peking by the Benedictines. However, apart from some emphasis in the field of education, the mission work of the Church continued on an individual basis, each missioner in his own way trying to save as many souls as possible. Not until World War I, when Benedict XV and his successor, Pius XI, took personal interest in the Church in China, was any attempt made to evaluate the Church's over-all mission policy.

In addition to this outline of the Catholic Church's activities in China prior to Maryknoll's entrance into the field, it is necessary to review—again, briefly—another phase of China's experience with the West.

Simultaneously with the sixteenth-century missioners, European commerce made contact with China. The early traders who came to China were hardly representative of Christian Europe's culture. Interested solely in profit, the vast majority attempted to amass as great a fortune and as quick a gain as possible, by any means, fair or foul. The unfavorable impression these Christian merchants made on the Chinese resulted in a major handicap to the Church and to future trade between China and the West.

The commercial adventurers from Europe were totally ignorant of China's ancient culture. Knowing nothing of her elaborate ceremonials, they ignored the customs of Chinese etiquette, even though they were ordered by the proud Chinese to study and learn the proper ritual before presenting themselves to an official. For example, people of inferior status were expected to perform the "kow-tow" before their superiors—kneeling and touching the forehead to the floor or ground. The kow-tow was considered humiliating by the Westerners and they refused to comply. The Chinese, in turn, regarded them as uncouth barbarians. There was constant friction. Furthermore, the Chinese felt that China had no particular need for trade with the West; that nothing was to be gained by it. For the most part they wanted to be left alone, and they could point to the Great Wall of China as the enduring monument to that desire.

But neither Chinese ceremonials, nor Chinese indifference, nor even the Great Wall could deter the eager merchants in their pursuit of profit. As early as 1557, in the first of many land grabs perpetrated against China, the Portuguese managed to obtain the "lease" of Macao. They needed a place, they said, to "dry their goods before they could be respectably presented to China." Portugal still enjoys the use of this piece of territory on China's southeast coast, forty miles below Hong Kong.

By the time the first American clipper ship, the *Empress of China*, sailed to the Orient in 1784, the British had already established a virtual trade monopoly in China. To the British trade was a right they could demand; to the Chinese, it was a privilege to be granted or withheld. The Chinese regarded the British as barbarians from a remote, insignificant, uncivilized island. The British disparagingly referred to the Chinese ignorance of international law, protocol and diplomatic procedures practiced in the West. Unfortunately there were no Jesuits in court to mitigate the issue.

Obviously, the cultural conflict was grave; the consequent misunderstanding was irreconcilable. It seemed that the problems could be solved only by military strength as each side insisted on the soundness of its position and values. The Opium War (1839–1842) served the purpose perfectly. This was the first of many military engagements between China and western powers in modern times.

It was the Portuguese from Goa who made the first shipment of opium in quantity to China. By 1729, about 25,000 pounds were imported annually. At that time the Chinese government issued a decree prohibiting the opium traffic. A century later, when war with Britain began, some four million pounds were being brought to China each year in Western ships.

Lin Tse-hsü, the Imperial Commissioner who was sent from Peking to Canton in 1839 to suppress the opium traffic, wrote to Queen Victoria: "In your honorable, barbarian country the people are not permitted to inhale the drug, how can selling it to us be reconciled with the decrees of heaven?" Another Chinese official charged: "Our country is becoming poorer and poorer and its people weaker and weaker." For the Chinese, the Opium War was a moral issue and they had no choice but to fight. The appalling aspect of the conflict was that a "pagan" country had thus to protect itself from Christian nations that insisted on breaking a militarily weaker country's laws and debilitating its people, because "opium was an important source of revenue."

In London Parliament debated the issue. Many members were horrified that Great Britain should go to war to compel the Chinese to accept the opium trade. William Gladstone (later Prime Minister) said at one point in the debate: "I will ask the noble Lord a question: 'Does he not know that the opium smuggled into China comes exclusively from British ports? . . . The great principles of justice are involved in this matter. You will be called upon to show cause for your present intention of making war upon the Chinese. They gave us notice to abandon the contraband traffic. When they found that we did not, they had the right to drive us from their coasts. . . . I am not competent to say how long this war may last, but this I can say, that a war more unjust in its origin, a war more calculated in its progress to cover this country with permanent disgrace, I do not know."

The Opium War was followed by other engagements with the powerful Europeans. China's resistance collapsed. The extent of her feebleness was revealed to the world. "Foreign concessions" were hacked out of the large coastal cities; large tracts of land, such as Hong Kong, Kowloon, and Kwangchowan were ceded or leased to Western nations by what China understandably refers to as the "unjust treaties." A clause of particular interest to our story was inserted in the 1858 treaty of Tientsin which followed China's defeat by the French and British in that city. (The war was provoked when a French missioner was killed in the interior of China.) Among other concessions demanded by the conquerors was the article in the treaty guaranteeing by the Chinese government protection for all Christian missioners, since "the Christian religion, as professed by Protestants and Roman Catholics, inculcates the practice of virtue and teaches man to do as he would be done by."

In the nineteenth century, colonialism constituted a European monopoly extending over a vast area of the world. This imperialism was justified by the colonial powers as being necessary for propagating a kind of life they considered superior. The real motive, of course, was the quest for power and profit.

It seemed almost as if the smoke from European factories and steamer funnels blinded the adventurers to the possibility of other civilizations and other cultures. They made no attempt to understand these cultures, nor did they consider the national pride of the people they subjected. By superior firepower all physical obstacles were easily overcome. Human obstacles, however, were quite another thing.

The spread of Christianity was not aided by these merchants and soldiers from Christian countries. Their conduct frequently shocked the "pagan" Chinese as they carried into the Orient their national and religious rivalries. The European governments controlled the Chinese Maritime Customs; they unjustly demanded concessions, insisting on special treatment: extraterritorial rights for their nationals and protection for their citizens who were in China propagating Christianity. China, strictly speaking, was not a colony of any one Western power; it was exploited as a colonial field open to all. China was what Sun Yat-sen called "not a colony, but a hypercolony."

What, as a matter of principle, was the Catholic Church's attitude toward colonialism? There is no question that in theory the Church did not recognize a "colonial" Christianity. The Church is a mystical body, having no "mother country." The Catholic religion is the same everywhere, with no country or civilization having the right to proclaim itself the elect of Christ or the vehicle of His message. Every Christian following the divine command has the duty to take an active part in the apostolate. For this reason, in their zeal many European monarchs, along with their colonizers and armies, felt it their responsibility to help send out missioners and to build churches and monasteries in the territories they annexed. There were, however, Catholics who opposed not only colonial abuses inflicted on native peoples, but also the whole system of colonization. Such a person was Bartolomé de las Casas, the champion of the American Indian. Unfortunately, Asia had no las Casas. And the Belgium missioner Père Vincent Lebbé, who became not only an apostle, but, through naturalization, a son, had not yet arrived on the China scene.

The Dominican friar, Francisco di Vittoria (died 1546) is considered one of the great masters of Catholic thought on the subject of colonization. Stated simply, his thesis maintained that all men are united by an original solidarity. The earth and all it contains belonged in the beginning to all men . . . this initial and common destiny remains fundamental . . . the colonizing state must govern the colony in such a way that it gradually comes to be able to guide its own affairs and to participate in the life of international intercourse and fellowship. His point of view displeased many European monarchs when it was published even though approved by the Church.

If some of her members exploited the people of colonial and semicolonial lands, they did so no doubt with the knowledge, but without the official endorsement, of the Church. The missioner was to have no part in the quest for land and profits.

It seems evident that from the beginning of the modern era of colonization the authorities in the Church and the civil authorities of the colonizing country had very different notions about the role of the missioner in the colonies, even though one Catholic foreign mission society in Europe was called the "colonial seminary." For example, there is a French Government document on the Paris Society of Foreign Missions, prepared in 1802 by M. Portalis, the French Councillor of State for Religion. "Missionaries," it states, "have carried the glorious name of France to the ends of the earth, extended France's influence and built up links with peoples whose very existence was unknown."

However, it is interesting to read what Bishop de Guébriant, a former Superior General of the Paris Foreign Mission Society had to say on this matter: "In the colonies, as elsewhere," he writes, "the missioners have only one aim which excludes any other: to convert pagan countries to Christianity . . . It is an illusion to think that Catholic missioners seek, or ever have sought, to ensure that the peoples whom they evangelize pass under or stay under white domination. . . . Whether the imputation is meant as praise or blame, it is quite simply false." Certainly de Guébriant and Portalis were not speaking the same language. As late as 1931, Gabriel Hanotaux in his work, *The Civilizing and Scientific Work of Catholic Missionaries in the French Colonies*, defined the missioner as the "predestined agent of a civilizing Empire."

In the eyes of most Chinese, Christian missioners appeared in the same light as Western merchants and soldiers —all Westerners coming to China from the colonial powers to exploit them. It is true there were similarities: all had servants, all lived, by comparison with their people, rather comfortably. It is also true that the missioner lived closer to the people than other foreigners, that he spoke their language, if not well, at least better, that he remained longer, and sought no personal gain. But, unfortunately, only a few of the Chinese people could see the difference.

There was another obstacle in the missioner's path toward the Christianization of China. The Chinese were not favorably impressed by the painfully contentious, frequently scandalous, diversity among the Christian churches. Orientals considered this a sign of inner weakness.

As England and France were enlarging their commerical interests in China and consolidating their territorial acquisitions, Russia was reaching out across Siberia demanding concessions and special privileges for her traders and for the representatives of the Russian Orthodox Church. In the far south, France, using the hostile attitude of the people toward French Catholic missioners as a pretext, annexed

Cochin China. Next Cambodia became a French protector-ate, and France had at last succeeded in laying the founda-tion of a Far Eastern empire. China for centuries had considered these "dependent states" under her control; they had paid annual tribute to China and the Chinese emperor invested their kings.

In 1897 when two German missioners were murdered in Shantung by Chinese robbers, Germany moved troops into Kiaochow Bay and, in the spirit of the day, demanded a ninety-nine year lease on the area. It is of interest to note that the peacemakers at Versailles, after World War I, granted this former German concession to—of all nations—Japan. Lou Tseng-Tsiang, the Chinese representative at Versailles, walked out of the treaty conference room and refused to sign the document. (Lou Tseng-Tsiang later became a Benedictine monk and died in a Belgium abbey shortly after World War II.) Ten thousand students in Peking, protesting against the Versailles Treaty, marched to the American Legation Quarters to ask the American representative to secure justice for China. When he refused to see them, the furiously angry students shouted "treach-ery."

The high-handed activities of the Western powers caused deep resentment in the hearts of most Chinese, par-ticularly among the officials and students. Unquestionably the Christian missioner was included in this antagonism. He too was an empire builder in the eyes of the Chinese. En-joying diplomatic immunity, backed by the military might of the West, the missioner was looked upon as a "foreign agent," as part of the advance guard of his country; behind him loomed the frightening hulk of a warship. When the Chinese Boxers gave vent to their pent-up hatred at the end of the nineteenth century, they unmercifully fell upon Christian missioners and their Chinese converts; they burned churches, mission schools, and hospitals as well as foreign legations. Anger long suppressed and misery long endured were not likely preparations for balanced reflection or moderate action. The inevitable consequence of having the military might of the Western powers descend upon them did not deter the Boxers. But there was no force in China at that time capable of offering resistance and so the Boxer Rebellion was subdued. For a moment it seemed that China as an independent nation was doomed. However, as one Chinese historian explains it, "China escaped annihilation because the Christian nations could not agree among themselves as to the manner of dividing our country."

Is it any wonder that the Christian missioner enjoying extraterritorial rights, not always well trained, seldom articulate in the difficult Chinese language, was, despite the charitable institutions that he established, considered by many intellectual Chinese an arm of Western aggression and imperialism? It would be difficult for the Church convincingly to disentangle its thread from the skein of responsibilities involved in colonial enterprises. Toynbee put it bluntly: "The West is being cited before the tribunal of history: Africans, Asians, Latin Americans are brought forward to denounce the West as the aggressor par excellence of modern times. If we understood this, it might have shaken our feeling of superiority or our pride by confronting us with a part we are all too apt to forget, or worse, to glorify."

The Holy See, except for Propaganda's farsighted document of 1659, remained silent about the global mission of the Church all through this era of European colonial expansion. Despite the founding of many new mission societies, there was not one encyclical that dealt with the subject of foreign missions. When *Rerum Novarum* was published in 1891, the missionary hierarchy did not see that its plea for better working conditions for the laborer was a fundamental document applying as much to China as it did to Europe. "What is shameful and inhuman is to use man as a vile instrument of gain." These words of Leo XIII were applied to Europeans and Americans who were exploiting the Chinese; however, the document was not implemented, and so the champion of the laboring man in China was not the Church, but the Bolsheviks and, later, the Communists.

In 1940, Monsignor (later Cardinal) Celso Constantini, Secretary of the Congregation of Propaganda, commented on the progress of the Church in China. "In the Far East," he said, "we founded not the Church with its normal structure, but the foreign missions, and Asia has not been converted." He contrasted this with the apostolic age of the primitive Church: "The apostles and missionaries of the sub-apostolic age founded the Church with an indigenous clergy and they converted the Western world. The experience of the past four centuries has shown our methods to be more or less sterile. The missioners of that early period set up the Church with an ordinary local hierarchy, and for the liturgy they used whatever language they found in use on the spot. Three hundred years of labor in China won the missioner only the stigma, 'imperialist aggressor,' 'foreign devil.'"

Bishop Francis Xavier Ford of Maryknoll died bearing the stigma of "imperialist aggressor," and "foreign devil," after a lifetime devoted to bringing Christ's salvation to the Chinese people whom he loved. Yet of all men, he especially endeavored to give living reality to the Propaganda document issued in 1659: "Do not take our countries to them, but the faith; that faith that does not repulse or offend the rites and customs of a country . . . but on the contrary desires that they should be preserved and protected."

❀ The Pagoda and The Cross

Grant us, Lord, to be the doorstep by which the multitudes may come to worship Thee. And if, in the saving of their souls, we are ground underfoot and spat upon and worn out, at least we shall have served Thee in some small way in helping pagan souls; we shall have become the King's Highway in pathless China.

FRANCIS X. FORD

 # CHAPTER I

CONFUCIUS

If upon looking into my heart I find that I am right,
I will go forward though those who oppose me
number thousands and tens of thousands.

ANALECTS 12.4.3

JESUS CHRIST

Amen I say to you, there is no one who has left
house, or parents . . . for the sake of the kingdom
of God, who shall not receive much more in the present
time, and in the age to come life everlasting.

LUKE 18:29–30

The Irish Fords

In 1846, the grandparents of Francis Ford left their beloved Ireland with three sons and one daughter, escaping the famine that threatened the family. Although the four men fought for their new homeland during the Civil War (one son lost his life aboard the *Cumberland* when it was sunk by the Confederate ironclad *Merrimac*), sympathy for the tribulations of the Irish people throughout the world permeated their lives. After the war, Austin Ford, the father of Francis, became publisher of the *Irish World* and editor of *The Freeman's Journal*. A dedicated champion of Irish freedom, he wrote fiery editorials that stirred the hearts of Irishmen everywhere. In fact, at one time it was a penal offense in British-controlled Ireland and in England to possess a copy of Ford's publication, which had a peak circulation of over one million.

The *Irish World* vigorously supported many worthy causes, and its editorials pressed for such labor reforms as an eight-hour working day, work compensation laws, and many of the "fringe benefits" taken for granted today.

Austin Ford possessed uncommon perceptivity and a sensitive feeling for the underdog, characteristics he transmitted to his son, Francis. He could not be a mere onlooker at injustice, a callous observer of suffering humanity. In his bitter fight for Irish freedom, he sought to rectify what he considered an unjust situation. In his tireless efforts on behalf of the working man, he was years ahead of his time, as later his son would be in the vanguard of American Catholic missioners in China.

The mother of Francis Ford, Elizabeth Anne Rellihan, was born on a farm in Keokuk, Iowa, in 1854. Her father had been a railroad man when the "iron horse" first pushed into Des Moines, but later he had turned to farming on the rich Iowa plains. Elizabeth Anne, when still a small girl, was kidnapped and held for a short time by a band of roving Indians. The experience helped her to identify with the pioneer people she loved and to emulate the stoic, yet adventuresome, spirit she admired.

An avid reader, the young Elizabeth eagerly devoured the pages of the *Irish World*, and as her writing competence increased she became a regular contributor to it. In 1876 she accepted Austin Ford's invitation to take a place on the editorial staff. The following year Austin Ford and Elizabeth Anne Rellihan were married. They established their household at 432 Carleton Avenue in Brooklyn.

Austin and Elizabeth Anne Ford's sixth child was born prematurely on January 11, 1892. Because he was not expected to live, preparations for his baptism were hurriedly arranged. In a short autobiography written twenty years later, Francis Ford wrote: "I narrowly escaped being called 'Christopher Columbus' owing to his centenary year in 1892, the year I was born. However, I was named in Baptism for St. Francis Xavier. No one in the family bore the name before. Shortly before my baptism my father had finished reading the life of St. Francis Xavier and was so impressed by his personality that he named me in honor of the Saint." How prophetic that Austin Ford should have selected the name of the great Basque Jesuit, apostle to the Orient!

Austin Ford was as strongly devoted to his religious life as he was devoted to his family and his writing. He was of the school that inspired "respect with a heavy dose of reverential fear." In his children he instilled a high regard for the value of prayer and a deep love of learning; and he was as much concerned with the duties of children to parents as he was with those of parents to children.

The home over which Austin Ford presided has been described by John Considine, who visited the household during the 1915 Christmas holidays, when he and young Ford were fellow seminarians. "Frank and I arrived just before supper and sat quietly through the meal, speaking only when spoken to, almost all the questions being put to Mr. Ford at the head of the table. After supper, Mr. Ford led us into the living room and took from his heavily loaded bookshelves Shakespeare's *Merchant of Venice*. We and the members of the household sat in a circle about the room as the old man, in what to me was a most interesting fashion, discoursed on the play and read us selected passages.

For poor Frank, however, it was his first night back with his brother and his sister, Una. He sat next to Una and soon the two, very much attached, were whispering excitedly to each other. But not for long. The father lifted his grave face from his book, stared at the son and said quite solemnly: 'Francis, are you listening?' 'Yes, father,' replied Frank very respectfully. The *Merchant of Venice* received undivided attention henceforth."

If Austin Ford was temperamentally on the severe side, his wife Elizabeth was a quiet, gentle person who never permitted her many responsibilities to ruffle her. As well as caring for her large family, she managed to attend Mass daily and to continue work on Mr. Ford's publications. Frank Ford often recalled how busily she wrote even while the children were eating breakfast. Besides writing for the *Irish World* and *The Freeman's Journal*, she prepared a daily column on Irish matters for the *New York Times*. She also found time to translate from the French a life of St. Joan of Arc and other works.

In this intellectually stimulating atmosphere, further enhanced by visits to the family residence from renowned writers and lecturers who contributed in some way to the Ford publications, Francis Ford grew up.

Frank Ford was in almost every way a typical American lad. He was known to have scratched his initials on his desk-top in school; boyhood acquaintances recall that he frequently mimicked the foreign accents of some of Brooklyn's latest arrivals from Europe. He liked dancing and was rather good at it, although he disliked dancing with his sister. Years later, he spoke about teaching some Chinese schoolboys two Irish reels for a dance contest in Kaying. He said: "It's a shame that the one talent I have [dancing] goes to waste over here."

When Frank was twelve, a bearded European missioner came to preach in Brooklyn. Years later, Ford recalled that Sunday morning. Dangling his feet over the edge of the boys' gallery of the old brick parish church, fascinated by the missioner's broken English and wild gestures, he listened in rapt attention. "He was Father Conrardy," Ford wrote, "a fiery enthusiast with a grizzly beard; his subject was his life work among Chinese lepers. He gloried in his work for them and flung the challenge in our face to show our Catholicity by helping him to build a home for these outcasts. It seemed harder for him to beg for money than to do the disgusting work of nursing slowly rotting Chinese men and women. . . . With a generous impulse I put a nickel in the basket, five times my usual sum. And the rest of the Mass was spent repeating to myself Father Conrardy's last words: 'My one ambeesch is to be a martyr.' "

The zealous leper priest became Ford's ideal. Although it is not possible to determine at what precise period of his life Frank Ford decided to become a priest, the mission talk was definitely the deciding factor in his determination to become a foreign missionary priest.

Francis Ford idolized his mother and confided in her throughout his school days, yet he did not tell her his thoughts about his mission vocation until he was certain it was to be his life's work. He did, however, discuss the matter with his confessor and counselor, Father Thomas Molloy (later Archbishop of Brooklyn), who had encouraged Francis in his priestly vocation. Molloy supported him completely in his desire to be a foreign missionary priest, although in 1908 such a desire was extraordinary for an American Catholic boy. (There was, for example, no missionary society in the United States, and but an isolated handful of American priests engaged in overseas missions. Furthermore, with the shortage of priests in America, the clergy was not enthusiastic about young men leaving the country for a foreign mission field. The American Catholic Church had too many parochial problems on its mind to find time to think very far beyond its parish walls.) In spite of his support and encouragement, however, Father Molloy insisted that Ford first complete his course at Cathedral College, an institution which at that time combined a four-year high school program with a two-year liberal arts college course for young men who were thinking of the priesthood.

Bishop Philip Furlong, at present auxiliary bishop of New York, was a classmate of Francis Ford at Cathedral. "I sensed," he says, "that somehow he was an exceptional person. He had a much greater intellectual capacity than the average student. We all knew he was highly gifted. In mathematics he acted as tutor for the class. He didn't bother much with competitive sports, although he was always on hand to cheer on the teams. He confided in me his interest in the foreign missions."

In 1912, less than a year after Maryknoll was established as the Catholic Foreign Mission Society of America, its founders visited Cathedral College. In the December 1960 issue of the *Cathedralite*, Bishop Furlong described their visit as the dramatic turning point of Francis Ford's life.

I met two priests as I was going downstairs. They were looking for the office of the Propagation of the Faith, which in those days was located on the first floor of Cathedral College. They tried the door. It was locked. I said to one of them: "I think the office is closed for the night,"—it was after five—"and I don't think you will be able to get in." The three of us started down the stairs to the street. The shorter of the two priests said to me: "I am Father Walsh and this is Father Price and we are founding a missionary seminary for the foreign mission." "Is that so?" I said, then excitedly added, "well, there's a boy in my class who's greatly interested in the foreign missions." They wished to know who he might be and I said, "his name is Frank Ford."

So I ran back to the top floor where my classmates were busy working on the school paper, *Cathedral College Chimes*, of which Ford was the editor. I said, "Frank, I just met two priests who are starting a missionary seminary." He wanted to know who they were and where they were. Eagerly he put on his coat and took off on the run after them. When last I saw him, he was disappearing down Madison Avenue.

"Suddenly," Father Walsh later wrote, "I felt a hand on my arm and turning found that a young man had been hastening after us from Cathedral College . . . He was a student of the senior class who gave his name as Frank Ford. He indicated he wished to enroll as an aspirant for the foreign missions. Whether he sensed my joy or not, I do not know, but it was unbounded, because Francis Ford was our first applicant and I felt exultant." On his return to Hawthorne, N.Y., the temporary quarters of the Catholic Foreign Mission Society, Walsh thanked God for so promising a candidate. "And now today I thank Him also because I have never for a moment had reason to doubt the perseverance of our first aspirant, and I have never thought of him otherwise than as faithful to the end, a fine priest, a zealous missioner and a loyal Maryknoller."

Francis Ford decided that everything must be settled before he broke the news to his parents. His mother simply asked him how long he had been thinking about the foreign

7

missions (she had already supported his decision to enter the priesthood). When he told her that it had been on his mind for a long time, that he had been inspired by Father Conrardy's mission talk and by reading the lives of St. Francis Xavier and Théophane Vénard, she consented and agreed to tell his father, who had opposed his original choice. As the young seminarian wrote in his autobiography, "My father very much doubted my firmness and good judgment when he learned that I was thinking about the priesthood. ... He wanted me to take my place in his office. Had not my mother opposed him almost weekly for a year, I would probably have discontinued studying."

The idea of allowing his son to become a foreign missioner was even more unthinkable to Austin Ford, and he sought to dissuade him. The autobiography continues:

> After rosary that night my father told me to remain with him and we talked it over until two in the morning. He was adamant. He could not give his consent. He said he was getting old (he was sixty-nine then) and had hoped I would take his place in the office . . . he argued that a Catholic newspaper could do more than five missioners in saving souls . . . Pius X realized the value of the Catholic press . . . Father Walsh had no right to impose on young men . . . the missionary idea is all right in poetry . . . the field looks green from a distance . . . and so on. I told him he could spare one of his four sons for the altar and writing was not my strong point . . . my mother testified to that many times. As the clock struck two, he sent me off to bed —neither one of us willing to yield. Next morning at the office he called me to his desk for more talks. "You are nearly twenty-one," he concluded sadly, "and master of yourself. I have been counting all along on your help, but if you insist on going, I'll not stop you . . . but you go without my approval."

"I must follow what I believe is God's will" was the son's reply.

Once Ford had entered Maryknoll, his father did nothing positive to interfere with his son's vocation. He simply ignored the new state of affairs, almost refusing to recognize that Frank had left home and certainly never realizing that he himself had fostered the dedication with which his son pursued the priesthood. One evening when he was with Frank in the family library, he had taken down a book on the life of St. Francis Xavier. He called his son over and said, "Francis, read this book. Here is a man for you. Be a man like this."

Maryknoll

Until the turn of the century, theology—dogmatic and moral—was the paramount concern of the Church leaders in Rome. The Church was universal in intention, to be sure, but only five percent of the Church's personnel and energy was spread over the vast non-Christian population. As late as 1908, the Church in Rome considered the United States to be a "mission country." As such, the American Church was directly responsible to the Prefect of Propaganda in the same manner as was China, or one of the primitive islands of the South Seas. The American hierarchy and priests, therefore, were concerned primarily, and almost exclusively, with the building of the Church within the national boundaries. Here and there, individual bishops and priests might have concerned themselves with global issues; but in general, any interest in Church affairs beyond the parish was limited to the particular mother country from which the immigrant had derived. Events in Ireland, for instance, were of great interest to many American Catholics, just as they were to Austin Ford. A few

American Catholics interested themselves in the foreign missions to the extent of sending small donations of money through their local diocesan Propagation of the Faith office. Parochial school children added cancelled stamps and rolls of tinfoil, and from time to time they would "ransom" a Chinese baby for five dollars. Otherwise the millions of people in Asia and Africa were rarely given a second thought.

If Christ's command "Go into the whole world and preach the gospel to every creature" was seemingly overlooked by most of Catholic America during the decades prior to World War I, the Protestant Churches were busy elevating the divine command into a primary article of faith. There was a vigor and a self-confidence in the Protestant missionary movement that was typified by the motto of the intercollegiate Student Volunteers for Foreign Missions: "The Evangelization of the World in this Generation." It would be rare to find this spirit on the American college campus today: it would have been rarer to find that global spirit in a Catholic college when Maryknoll was beginning.

Frank Ford recorded the reaction among his fellow college students in the spring of 1912 when he mentioned to his table companions that he had signed up for the new mission seminary at Maryknoll. "Eating stopped," he recalled, "and there were shouts of protest backed by the thought that I had lost my reason." Then he added: "Had that been a class in a Protestant college, intelligent sympathy with the mission cause would have prompted instant congratulations."

It is amazing to read of the recklessness with which outstanding young Protestants of that day flung themselves into this Christian foreign mission crusade. China was the great magnet that drew them to the mission cause in those days. That generation had no squeamish doubts about the superiority of the American way of life. They wanted to share this "good life" and enlighten the "dark world of heathenism."

After World War I, however, Protestant mission efforts encountered serious difficulty. For a few years the number of volunteers for overseas work increased slightly as did the amount of contributions. But in 1926, the declining interest in the church caught up with the overseas mission efforts. In that year the number of Protestant students who decided to become missionaries was less than half the number six years earlier. In 1920, 1,731 new missionaries went abroad; in 1927, only 538 made the voyage to new mission posts. In 1920, 2,783 had signed the Student Volunteer pledge; but by 1925, the number had dropped to 764, and in 1928 to 252. State and private universities and colleges that had only tenuous demoninational connections had provided a large number of the Protestant missionary candidates—even in some secular institutions there was an atmosphere conducive to the development of missionary interest. But this environment changed. Paul A. Varg in his book, *Missionaries, Chinese and Diplomats*, cites Williams College as an example. Famous as the birthplace of the American missionary movement, Williams could not claim a single Volunteer between the years 1926 and 1930.

[In recent years, the decline among Protestant missionary groups has reversed. Today there are over 30,000 U.S. Protestant missioners in the field, divided almost equally in Asia, Africa, and Latin America.]

During the golden era of American Protestant foreign mission effort, little was being done overseas by the American Catholic Church. In the United States at that time there were but a few fund-raising centers of the Society for the

Propagation of the Faith. To one of its offices, in Boston, Archbishop O'Connell had appointed Father James Anthony Walsh as the director.

Walsh, who was to become the co-founder of Maryknoll, had plunged into the work of making the American Catholic Church mission-minded. He was convinced that the Christian Church should not be primarily pastoral, that her first concern must be her missionary character. Father Walsh realized that what is unknown does not attract. "Every cause should have a literature," he believed; and in order to bring the foreign missions to the attention of American Catholics, to arouse sympathy for and understanding of the mission cause, he decided to publish a magazine. He modeled it after the most popular and successful secular magazines of that time and called it *The Field Afar*.

About the time that *The Field Afar* was being launched in Boston, another American priest, Father Thomas Frederick Price, was having some thoughts of his own about foreign missions. He wrote in his diary in 1907: "One thing has come to me with force . . . the foreign mission development is the true and full end of my work."

Price had founded a magazine in 1897 that bore the name *Truth*. Through the magazine he expressed his conviction that the proper task of the Church was not only to care for and nourish the membership at home, but to convert the world to Christianity. In the May 1906 issue of *Truth*, he wrote about the need of a foreign mission seminary:

> Such a seminary ought to be established around the Catholic University in Washington, and it should have preparatory schools in all our large Catholic centers— in New York, in Boston, in Philadelphia, in Chicago, in St. Louis, and in San Francisco. With these prepara-

tory schools all over the country as feeders, there would spring up an ideal of sacrifice for our Faith, there would be an outlet for the generosity of souls that would soon have the most far-reaching effects not only on ourselves, but on the foreign mission work of the world. . . .

(Although Maryknoll was eventually established thirty miles north of New York City and not in Washington, Father Price's 1906 vision has found realization. Today Maryknoll does have preparatory schools in or near the precise centers he suggested.)

When Father Walsh read the May 1906 *Truth* article, he hastened a note to Father Price: "The foreign mission seminary idea has also been very close to my heart. Speed the day when it may arrive! I believe that the time is well ripe."

Gradually working toward the same end, the one in Boston, the other in North Carolina, the two priests exchanged their ideas in occasional correspondence. And how similar those ideas were! In 1909, Father Price wrote in *Truth*:

It has always been a subject of regret that so little has been known or studied about foreign missions among our Catholic people. Even among priests and educated Catholics there is very little knowledge of this subject. With the exception of the *Annals of the Propagation of the Faith* and some other papers founded for the local purpose of collecting money and a few missionary biographies, our literature on the subject is meager. The object of the Catholic Church is to convert the world—to teach all nations—but before all nations can be taught, they should be studied and every effort should be bent to warm every Catholic heart to the work. In every parish, in every school and academy and university, the work should go on unremittingly—in study, in prayer and in work. "Thy Kingdom come" should be a continuous cry welling up from every human heart. There should be mission textbooks for every school, and more scientific works for the learned. . . . At the present time, however, we fear that even priests would be embarrassed if they were asked for an account of foreign mission work. . . .

The Church in the United States is sending out almost no missioners to foreign countries. In a few years this is likely to change. We look to the Catholics of the United States to become the great mission force in the world, and therein lies the salvation of the Church in the United States. . . .

In September 1910, Father Price attended the Eucharistic Congress in Montreal. When he learned that the editor of *The Field Afar* was also present at the Congress, he contacted Father Walsh and they arranged to meet. The two priests were utterly oblivious of the hustle and bustle going on about them in the hotel lobby. They talked and talked. There in Montreal they formulated the plan to establish a foreign mission society in the United States.

Father Price was well known to many members of the American hierarchy who, with him, had attended St. Charles College and St. Mary's Seminary in Baltimore. He approached Cardinal Gibbons of Baltimore who enthusiastically endorsed the project and proposed the idea to all the members of the American hierarchy: "A seminary for foreign missions such as that contemplated," he said, "if established with the good will of the entire American hierarchy, can hardly fail to draw, emphatically, the attention of American Catholics to the cry that comes from one thousand million souls, who, as yet, have not heard Christ's message."

In his letter to the American hierarchy, Cardinal Gibbons, after observing "we are still short of priests in many dioceses," goes on to quote the words of Cardinal Manning, founder of the Mill Hill Mission Society in England: "It is quite true that we have need of men and means at home, and it is *because* we have need of more men and more means than we as yet possess, that I am convinced we ought to send both men and means abroad. . . ."

After securing the encouragement of the American hierarchy and having the permission of their own bishops, the organizers were advised to visit the most important foreign mission seminaries in Europe and then to proceed to Rome for the authorization necessary to start. Cardinal Gibbons outlined a few of the guidelines they were to follow once the two founders returned to the States. With the approval of the individual bishops, they were: (1) to secure spiritual aid . . . (2) spread a knowledge of the missions . . . by an output of mission literature . . . (3) seek material support, chiefly by increasing the subscription list of *The Field Afar*.

Fathers Walsh and Price reached Rome on a Sunday evening in June. For ten days they called on various Vatican officials. On Thursday morning, June 29, 1911, Cardinal Gotti informed the two Americans that the Propaganda Council was most favorably disposed toward their petition and gave them permission to begin the work, authorizing them to purchase land and a house and to appeal for students.

The next day they were received by Pope Pius X. The Holy Father read carefully the four page schema and, observing that the Council of Propaganda had already given its approval, said: "Why, it is all settled!" He then blessed the priests and offered his prayers and best wishes for the success of the new enterprise.

The new seminary was to be established within fifty miles of New York City. But where? Cardinal O'Connell of Boston had strongly urged them to settle in his diocese. After all, Father Price was a close friend of the Cardinal and Father Walsh was a native of Boston, and had directed the Society of the Propagation of the Faith there. But Walsh had his eyes turned toward New York, the national and international center where the world converges.

A few days after returning from Rome, the two founders were in Washington to report to the Apostolic Delegate. Cardinal Farley, then archbishop of New York, was there for a ceremony. They asked him if he should like to have the new mission society established within the limits of the New York archdiocese. The Cardinal's reply was immediate and warm. With opened arms he spoke one word, "Welcome."

As soon as Dominican Father Cothonay, an old friend and Prior of Holy Rosary parish at Hawthorne, learned that they wished to establish in the New York area, he lost no time in extending hospitality to the organizers. He also suggested that he might be able to supply professors if and when they were needed. On October 20, 1911, Fathers Walsh and Price moved into an old frame house on Manhattan Avenue. They took their meals at the Dominican refectory. Today there is a granite monument in the Priory garden whose bronze tablet top bears the inscription: "Maryknoll, cradled here at Hawthorne, is everlastingly grateful to the Dominican Fathers for the hospitality given in the first days and grateful to the Sisters of the Rosary Hill Cancer Home for all their kindnesses, and grateful to the Archdiocese of New York for its welcome."

The infant society remained at Hawthorne ("our Bethlehem," as the founders referred to it) for almost a year. It was to this house that Francis Ford reported as the first Maryknoll student on September 14, 1912. The second student, James Edward Walsh (now a Maryknoll bishop imprisoned in Shanghai) arrived from Cumberland, Maryland, on September 15. And on September 18, the Society's headquarters moved to the new and permanent Maryknoll on a hilltop farm overlooking the Hudson River near Ossining, New York. The official diary of those days speaks of September 18 as a "raw evening when we left Hawthorne under cover of darkness so as to spare the feelings of the villagers. We had six miles to drive and into the carriage built for four, seven of us crowded with our baggage . . . We clung to oil lamps that were to give us the first heat and light in our new home; our hearts were glad."

James Edward Walsh wrote of those early days: "Maryknoll was more like a home in the country than a seminary . . . , life was more like that of an ordinary close-knit family than an institution." Perhaps it was this quality that sustained Frank Ford during his first months at Maryknoll, for two weeks after he entered there, his mother, his chief human support, suddenly and unexpectedly died. It was a severe shock to the young seminarian, yet his fellow students noticed that he said nothing about it and showed no emotion. He simply put on his street clothes and went alone to Brooklyn to attend the wake and funeral. When he returned to Maryknoll, he resumed his routine quietly. And thus his autobiography ended: "I give thanks to God especially for my mother who saw me through college and safely at Maryknoll where I have but to imitate those about me in order to please God."

James Edward Walsh recalled that Frank Ford adapted

himself to the strange, country-style, crowded conditions as if he had never known any other. Ford himself later confided that he rather welcomed the primitive conditions of the first Maryknoll at Hawthorne and the broken-down farmhouse at Ossining. "The pioneering atmosphere was a refreshing change," he said, "from the effete city life of Brooklyn and New York." And, after all, he rather expected that conditions would not be soft in a seminary designed to prepare men for foreign missions.

Conformity to seminary rules was not easy for Frank Ford, but he knew that organized community life demanded conformity of every member. He found that common privations strengthened the spirit of the young Society and bound its members together more firmly.

Father Considine recalling those days says: "The pioneering on the hilltop, where all was of the primitive observance, suited Frank Ford to a T. He got to know every corner of the fields and woods. He found a spot in the woods he labelled his 'cathedral' and to it he often stole with his books and his thoughts." (Throughout his life Ford had this innate yearning, this shyness, which made him prefer to go off in a corner and read or write. He had no wish whatever to represent this attitude as a virtue; on the contrary, he constantly fought his love for solitude and tried to make himself always approachable by throwing himself into the thick of problems and mingling with anyone who would discuss with him the mission message. Although he never completely retired within himself, he preferred to remain in the background, quietly directing and encouraging, letting others, whenever possible, stand in the spotlight.)

What manner of young man was Frank Ford that he would be the first to enter on the path of a Maryknoll seminarian, that he would assume the responsibility to bring Christ to the world? What was there in this slim young Brooklynite that made him defy his father's wish and take such a tremendous gamble? Part of the answer comes from the few men who were with him at Maryknoll during those pioneering years. Bishop Raymond A. Lane recalls how Ford had a way of walking fast, rather jauntily, and of talking fast. He relates, "It was clear to all of us that Frank Ford had a way also of thinking fast, and more often than not, correctly." He was shy but not aloof; his humor was quiet rather than raucous. His wit was spontaneous, never offensive; his manner informal, though never vulgar or overfamiliar. Frank Ford had a pleasantly striking—some thought debonair—face and dark eyes sparkling with shrewdness. His body was a trim and graceful five feet, ten inches in height. Though he was not physically robust and found manual labor in the missionary seminary difficult, he never refused a job no matter how taxing, nor did he ever indicate that he was tired. One of his contemporaries recalled, "He was always ready to pitch in when there was extra work to be done."

Frank Ford seemed a little more serious than the average student, a little less interested in competitive sports than his more robust companions. But he was, as Lane says, "in student pranks the equal to any of us."

Many who knew him as a student described him as "buoyant." But for all his buoyancy, there was a seed of melancholy in him, which he normally kept under control. He was humble and gentle in success, never depressed in honest failure, never hypnotized by the cult of novelty. There seemed to be in him a strange mixture of "quicksilver and syrup," a combination of sharp intellect and deep sentimentality. Some speak of his "dignified reserve," his seeming detachment; yet even the men who at first approached him with hesitation admitted that his personality left a deep impression.

Those who understood him best remember that Ford possessed a "special beauty of character," a "depth of feeling," a "thoughtfulness unusual in a young man." He had a special reverence for the Mother of Jesus and for all things holy. His humble simplicity allowed him to ignore superficiality and to overlook the rudeness and thoughtlessness of others. Always he exhibited an insight into the feelings of others. This "depth of feeling," observed by his associates in the seminary, became more evident as he later recorded his observations on Chinese life and the Chinese people among whom he lived. But even in those early years, those who looked beneath the buoyant air and smiling eyes could see the delicate sensitivity and responsiveness that permitted him to understand and sympathize with others.

Frank Ford completed with distinction his course of theology at Dunwoodie, the New York archdiocesan seminary in Yonkers, where Maryknollers studied before Maryknoll had its own professional staff. He was ordained to the sacred priesthood on December 15, 1917. Bishop Cusack of Albany conferred the sacrament of Holy Orders on three Maryknollers in the old farmhouse chapel.

The Maryknoll superior, Father James Anthony Walsh, was not at home for this memorable ceremony. He was in China seeking a field of missionary labor for his young American society. Incredible as it may seem, with less than one percent of the Chinese population Christian, and with a hopeless shortage of missioners for the overwhelming apostolic task, one after another the European bishops throughout north and central China had politely refused to give him territory. Though they may have been aware of the excellent work being done by American Protestant missioners, they thought the life of a missioner in China would be too difficult for comfort-loving Catholic Americans. But on Christmas Day, Walsh cabled an exciting message to the community at Maryknoll: "We have a mission." In the province of Kwangtung, the bishop of Canton had agreed to cut off the southern portion of his vast South China vicariate, and he gave it to the new, untried American missionary society.

After Father James Anthony Walsh returned from his long journey through the Orient to search out a territory for Maryknoll, he began making plans for the pioneer band that would leave for the new South China mission in the fall of 1918. Because of his mission experience, Father Price had asked to head the new endeavor. Even so, one can imagine the tense expectation in the little refectory when Father Walsh rose to announce the names of those who would compose the first group, dropping each name like a stone into the liquid silence. Thomas Frederick Price! James Edward Walsh! Bernard Meyer! Francis Xavier Ford! A modest start, but a milestone for the Catholic Foreign Mission Society of America.

A few days before the first departure ceremony, a large bronze bell arrived at Maryknoll. It had hung for countless years in a Japanese Buddhist temple before being given to Father Walsh when he visited Japan in 1917. Inscribed on the bell was a Buddhist poem that could very well be a missioner's prayer:

> Please bring light to the darkness;
> Please open the spiritual blindness. . . .

Through the years, the dull, solemn sound of the temple bell has signalled the start of the annual departure ceremony.

When for the first time the wooden mallet banged the bell on September 8, 1918, it sounded the challenge for Maryknoll priests to carry the gospel overseas. The superior, in a stirring talk to the four missioners, reminded them of their heavy responsibility as pioneers. European missioners he had met in the Orient had expressed little confidence that soft Americans could stand the complex demands of mission life. Money, yes; Americans would contribute funds, they felt, but would not commit their lives. Father Walsh was certain, however, that American youth would give its blood as well as its gold. "You are soldiers of Christ, as yet unknown, untested and in some respect lightly esteemed, as were the soldiers of our nation before their deeds of valor on the battlefields of Europe. You are yet to prove that faith, humility, self-denial and zeal are not lacking in American youth." He pointed out their missionary duties; the need for personal sanctification and a love of the Crucified, the need for a careful use of money and for a loyal union with the Society, and finally a love for the people they were to serve.

Following the address the superior slowly and reverently presented each of the four priests with his missioner's crucifix. Then on bended knee they read the *Propositum*, the solemn promise to remain for life in the service of the Society.

There was deep joy mingled with sadness as the community sang the Departure Hymn, a translation of the stirring composition written by Charles Gounod for the Paris Foreign Missioner Society: "Go forth, farewell for life, O dearest brothers. Proclaim afar the sweetest name of God. . . ." The seminarians then chanted the *Benedictus*, the Canticle of Zachary, the Church's fitting prayer for those setting out on a long journey: "For those shall go before the face of the Lord to prepare His ways . . . to enlighten those who sit in darkness and in the shadow of death."

The departing missioners lined up before the altar and one by one the members of the community approached to exchange with them the kiss of peace. Finally the four departants saluted Father Walsh, their superior. The first three did so warmly, but with ceremonial formality. It was Father Francis Ford whose feelings welled up and overflowed. Unabashedly he threw his arms about his superior and kissed him on both cheeks. The moment for him represented a lifetime severance with the one who had become to him a father in Christ.

The four missioners sailed out of San Francisco on September 21 on the SS *Ecuador*. As the ship passed through the Golden Gate, the little band of apostles gathered on the afterdeck and softly chanted the *Ave Maris Stella*. The outlines of California faded into the sea and soon they were beyond their native land heading for the great unknown. For a moment Frank Ford's heart was saddened by the sharp recollection of his father's face as he said goodbye. "Time," he had told his sister, "would reconcile Dad." Happily, he was right. In October of the following year Frank Ford's sister Una wrote the following note to Father James A. Walsh: "I know you will like to hear that with Francis' last goodbye my father's attitude toward his call to the priesthood suddenly and completely changed. In fact, his chief pleasure now is any word from or about Francis or the missions."

Alone on the deck of the *Ecuador*, Ford turned his gaze toward the Orient. He was both the adventurous young man and the selfless apostle giving his life to a great cause.

He could not have known then what it meant to give up the habits of his city and take on the habits of the simple peasant folk among whom he would live under the blazing South China sun, but he had the special grace of a missionary vocation, a yearning for distant lands and peoples, and a longing to tell those people about Christ.

The restless eagerness with which he sailed toward his lifelong task is well described in a poem he dedicated to the Pacific Ocean he was crossing:

> O depth of mystery
> How can you calmly sleep
> And sluggishly stretch your breadth
> Of shining, peaceful deep
> Between the Day and Night
> And God's all-saving Light?

✿ CHAPTER II

LAO TZU

To realize that our knowledge is ignorance is a noble insight.

TAO TEH CHING, LH 71

SAINT PAUL

I count everything loss because of the excelling knowledge of Jesus Christ, my Lord.

PHILIPPIANS 3:8

The Orient

Stopping for a few days in Japan, Francis Ford was delighted with the attractive, hospitable Japanese. He wrote to Maryknoll: "My love for the Japanese is growing alarmingly. . . . I don't know how to explain it, but I can realize our Lord's hunger for souls after walking through the streets of Tokyo . . . a city of over two million and so few Christians. . . . I should like to work here all my life. I hate to think of leaving Japan to go to save others. It's like ignoring a drowning man simply because there is another farther on in the same condition."

The neat dress, the polite manner, and the warm smiles of the Japanese surprised the young missioner. He expected everyone to be uncouth and "heathen," worshiping idols and living in pagan darkness.

In truth, little in his training had prepared him to see anything of merit in the culture and religious practices of the people he had come to serve. Oriental culture and philosophy had not been a part of his course of study. Not until he began to study the Confucian system of ethics and the doctrine of the T'ao, the lofty thoughts in Buddhism and the praiseworthy aspects of ancestor ceremonies, did he see that many so-called pagan rites were indeed religious acts.

In this ancient civilization, everything was startingly new to the young Father Ford. Every alley was a pathway to adventure.

Together Father Price and Father Ford traveled through Japan and North China. The European missioners they visited were hospitable but skeptical. Jokingly, veteran missioners in Shanghai told the Americans they would be on their way home inside a year.

The next port of call was Hong Kong.

A few days after reaching Hong Kong, Ford wrote a letter to Maryknoll revealing something of what he had expected to find: "We had visions of an irrepressible lot of coolies dropping our baggage almost anywhere—if they did not take off with it—and losing half of it in the bargain. But our arrival was expected. A member of the Paris Foreign Mission Society met us and took generous care of us. Our baggage was hoisted out of the hold, counted, identified and, after some directions by the French priest, it arrived safely at our destination. We began to realize that all was not as chaotic as it seemed—or as chaotic as we expected."

Ford was bewitched by the British Crown Colony's busy harbor with its toiling ferry boats shuttling back and forth, destroyers sleek as swordfish side by side, ocean liners exhaling their heavy smoke, and sampans gliding over the water like insects. But he tarried only a few days before setting out for Canton where he and Father Price met Fathers Meyer and James E. Walsh. From Canton the four Maryknollers travelled south by junk the 150 miles to their destination, Yeungkong, a town of about thirty thousand people in the hot humid southeast coastal area of Kwang-tung.

Twenty years before the Maryknollers arrived, a Paris Foreign Missioner had succeeded in developing a small community of Christians there. When he learned that the new American mission society had accepted the Yeung-kong territory, the French priest wrote succinctly to Mary-knoll: "The seed sprang up encouragingly until unfavorable circumstances interfered." Then he added with frank fore-boding: "Your missioners will have to work hard and they will have to suffer."

At midnight, one week before Christmas, 1918, the four American missioners entered the quiet town worn out from their long journey. Ford mentioned in his diary that they thought of cabling the news of their safe arrival back to Maryknoll, but when they found out it would cost fifteen dollars they decided to write. "We are all well and happy," he said, "and would not change places with anyone in the world." He found the place much better than ex-pected. The Christians had festooned the front of the Church, shot off strings of firecrackers, and prepared a special welcome dinner in their honor.

The Maryknollers' first Christmas in China was a memorable occasion. A few days after the feast, Father Price wrote back to Maryknoll: "Such a Christmas! A Christmas we never experienced nor conceived of in all our lives! The Christians made a gala day of it, pouring in on

Christmas Eve and all day Christmas in delegations from all the villages, celebrating both the Nativity and our arrival. . . . We had solemn Midnight Mass, Fathers Ford and Meyer formed the choir. The little church was filled. . . . It was a great day, such as we shall never again experience perhaps, and we thank God for it."

Father Price knew that the number of Christians was small and their influence negligible. He wanted to reach out and give the gospel message to all these people whom he admired so much: people "so industrious, peaceful and amiable." He saw them dying by the millions without faith in Jesus. And he felt anguish because priests were so few. "May God speed the work," he wrote, "not only of Maryknoll, but of all missionary societies of the world, in sending men and women to this field whose harvest is ripe unto whiteness."

In their cramped Yeungkong quarters Father Price occupied one room and, according to a letter from Ford, "Three of us are in the other room; luckily none of us snores." After a few weeks Father Gauthier of the Paris Foreign Mission Society, who had been the Yeungkong mission's pastor, departed and the Americans were on their own to answer sick calls and visit distant village mission stations.

The first few weeks of any new enterprise can be critical. For a person from the complex culture of the West to be dropped suddenly into a rural Chinese environment is like stepping backward in time, and there is always the danger of a disturbing cultural shock. Ford's attitude from the first day was fortunately a healthy, positive one of acceptance. His broad training for the priesthood had prepared him in self-discipline and humility. His deep, sensitive understanding made it possible for him to be patient with the shortcomings of others. The impact of whatever shock he experienced from the rather strong dose of cultural change was cushioned by his ability to adjust. He seemed to feel little of the anxiety that others experienced when faced with unusual and baffling situations.

This does not mean that in the beginning he suffered no frustrations or annoyances. He did, and he wrote about them: interminable delays in travel, exasperating stupidity, thoughtless interruptions at all hours, the discomfort of being stared at while eating and laughed at when bungling the strange language. Naturally these vexations irked him, as did the strange odors and sounds, the mosquitoes and flies, the relentless and oppressive heat. But none of these difficulties upset Ford's sense of humor nor his equilibrium. What was in the beginning unfamiliar and unpleasant, perplexing and annoying, soon became understandable and acceptable. And nearby was Sancian Island, offering him encouragement and inspiration in the thought of St. Francis Xavier, who died there, looking across the narrow strip of water from the bleak and deserted rocks toward the villages of the Yeungkong territory that he had hoped to evangelize.

Before the original band had completed one year in China, Father Price became critically ill and required urgent medical care. After he endured the long, tortuously slow trip from Yeungkong to Hong Kong under a blazing August sun, the doctors discovered that his appendix had burst. It was too late to save him.

Ford wrote sadly to Father Walsh at Maryknoll: "My sympathy goes out to you in the loss which will strike you harder than anyone else. . . . I feel our saintly 'Father Bernadette' will aid the Society now more than ever by his intercession for us. . . . I can't help envying his lifetime of preparation for meeting God. His room here will always be an inspiration for us to aim higher, or rather to trust more in God. . . ."

As he moved among the people, Ford realized that long hard hours must be spent studying the Chinese language with its difficult sounds and script if he hoped to transmit to the people his thoughts, his ideas, his message. The dialect used in the Yeungkong area was Cantonese. Although he found the language fascinating, he also found it extremely difficult to master and admitted in an early letter to Maryknoll that he didn't have a "good ear for it." Every free moment away from the demanding duties of mission work was spent with the language teacher. Even so, the lack of a formal language school, the pressures of mission work, and the tremendous gaps in his knowledge of Chinese culture caused Ford to get a rather bad start on the language. Experience has shown that unless a good beginning is made during the first two years, the language in all probability will never be spoken accurately and fluently. Language deficiencies may be balanced by other qualities in a missioner, but blunders often become a source of irritation or amusement to the listener. Certainly Ford was made aware of his shortcomings, for he later impressed upon young missioners in his charge the need for them to master the strange tongue. All things being equal, the Holy Spirit works far more effectively with a missioner who can express himself clearly and grammatically.

From the beginning, Ford realized that the little knowledge he had of China was inaccurate and prejudicial to the Chinese people and their culture. And after four years in China, he made a sad and humble confession of his ignorance in a letter to Maryknoll:

This may sound like incipient heresy, but I'm only just now discovering the civilization of China and falling in love with it . . . I must honestly confess that before I came here I did not know China was civilized. Our United States schoolbooks, I think, still classify China among the "semi-civilized nations." I knew she had antiquity . . . but to think that China was completely equipped with a literature and culture 3,000 years before our ancestors were civilized was a hard blow to an Irishman. And I'm still puzzled as to why our schoolbooks are silent on the matter.

Father Francis Ford had spent most of his life in America in the company of Catholics—his family, his school associates, his friends for the most part were all Catholic; his preparation for the priesthood was Western orientated. It is a tribute to his keen mind and his sensitive nature that he could understand so soon and so well the feelings and mind of the Chinese. Later on, as the Bishop of Kaying, he explained it this way: "The missioner so far as skin and tongue permit him, forgets that he is an alien; for he is not a mere sojourner in a strange land which would give him the outlook of a port city merchant or a colonial official." The misnomer "foreign missioner" he said, "separates the priest from his people."

Ford recognized that there were beautiful, honorable things in the traditional customs of the Chinese and in their religious rites. These whenever possible he would welcome and accept, confident that in the end they would contribute to the triumph of Christ. He consciously equated this position with St. Paul's great dictum: "Whatsoever things are true, whatever honorable, whatever just . . . if there be any virtue, if anything worthy of praise, think upon these things." For "all things work together unto good, for those

who love God," how much more those things that are just
and honorable?

But there were few missioners in China in those first
decades of this century who were sensitive to the positive
values in Confucian ethics, or in the remembrance of ancestors, or in the Buddhist doctrine Ford learned to appreciate.
Because of what he called "Western bias," he formed the
habit of leaning the other way in his conversation and in
his writing. As time went on, unconsciously he sided with
the Chinese, interpreting their actions favorably, loyally
defending their virtues. Most foreigners developed the
"hand washing complex" from a fear of picking up germs;
Ford would go to the opposite extreme and deliberately
touch persons or objects that seemed contaminated. Frequently foreigners went into a fit of anger over delays in
travel; Ford forced himself to relax patiently and chat with
the people. Having been told that every Chinese workman
and businessman might try to cheat him, he frequently displayed a confidence in them that bordered on imprudence.

Ford's fundamental cure for "cultural shock" was a
genuine love for the people and a display of personal interest in them. Visiting their homes, he found the Chinese
quite ready to talk about themselves and their families. As
he learned more about them and better understood their
traditions, it was easier for him to adapt and to accept these
new forms of behavior. For Francis Ford the encounter was
in terms of reverence, respect, and love, a meeting of
brothers.

Ford was aware of the enormous curiosity the Chinese had about life in America. He would try to satisfy
their interest honestly, without false vainglory, without
making any attempt to convert them to the "American
way of life," without making insidious comparisons between
China and his own country and ever careful not to empha-

size his country's physical power or to intimate that the United States had the right to force its views on others. He knew that China's staggering, complex problems—poverty, illiteracy, injustice, disease—could not be solved by force. Ford was, as one Maryknoll missioner put it, the ideal diplomat, for he showed at all times a genuine respect for his hosts. In the beginning he may have been unfamiliar with Chinese etiquette and ignorant of Chinese customs, but he never wantonly disregarded their age-old precepts, nor trampled underfoot their ancient conventions.

Foreign Devils

As the young pastor of the Yeungkong mission, Ford tried every possible means to convince the villagers that he really was happy to be amongst them. But Yeungkong was a difficult assignment. After the initial warm reception, the missioners found a less cordial atmosphere. The people were rigidly conservative, hard-working farmers, fishermen, and shopkeepers. They were provincial and narrow, wary of foreigners and novelties. The area had been hard on the previous Christian missioners. Prior to the Maryknollers' arrival, the American Protestant mission had been twice destroyed, despite the stern warning to the offenders from the provincial government at Canton, which was held responsible for the safety of the Christian missioners and for the damage done the Church.

Although he did not fully understand the reasons for it, Ford was conscious of the distant, at times antagonistic, attitude of the townspeople. Why did so many people call him "foreign devil"? He had come to China for no personal gain, why did they suspect him? He sensed that in the minds of many business men and students his presence was merely tolerated. In an attempt to gain good will he decided to construct a combination orphanage and clinic on a piece of land he was able to buy opposite the chapel and parish house left by the French Fathers. But even his charitable efforts were misunderstood. He heard of grotesque stories being spread about the mission: that many children were dying in the mission orphanage because the priests were eating the hearts and eyes of the infants; that people were being poisoned in the mission clinic; that kegs of gunpower (actually Mass wine) were being imported from America; that American and French gunboats plying the river were in constant touch with the missioners. From time to time students would demonstrate, marching through the streets with screaming placards: "Citizens, do you want to fall into the hands of the foreigner? Arise! Destroy the Christian Church! Kill the foreign devils!"

Only the slightest spark was needed to convert the nationalistic and anti-Christian sentiments into an organized crusade. When the China Continuation Committee published a book called *The Christian Occupation of China*, the smouldering resentment against Christian missioners burst into flames. The Anti-Christian Alliance was formed and, together with the influential Young China Society, bitterly attacked missioners and mission institutions.

In the spring of 1919 Ford wrote: "Eleven villages [in the Yeungkong district] were completely stripped of everything movable and all the water buffalo were driven off. The people in the rest of the district are so terrified that they are moving with all their belongings into the market town where the soldiers are stationed. The rice planting season has just begun, so it is going to go very hard with these people who, even in favorable times, can only just make a living."

In 1918 a Protestant missioner describing the conditions in Yeungkong wrote in a mission magazine: "Fighting in

Yeungkong ... between the local troops and some northern soldiers had led to such a serious situation the missionaries there sent to the American Consul at Canton for help. An American gunboat, then in Hong Kong, was sent to their relief." This was the normal recourse used by missioners when they were in physical danger. Actually, Ford himself in 1925—under obedience and reluctantly, it is true— was whisked off to Manila by an American gunboat when an uprising in Yeungkong and the entire Kongmoon area got completely out of control. The United States Consul in Canton had advised Monsignor James Edward Walsh to send all his priests out of China. Walsh, after prayerful thought, made the painful decision to follow the Consul's instruction. The young superior said: "I hated to do this, but I could see no use in having everybody butchered in a purely political trouble." When two years later European missioners discussed the incident in Rome and chided the Maryknollers for running away in fear at the first sign of danger, Monsignor Walsh indignantly protested that European missioners had been doing the same thing for years. He concluded: "In the future, I will not ask any of our men to leave until they are carried out on a stretcher."

The early 1925 incident was the first and only time Ford hid behind the American flag, and he was embarrassed later to recall the rescue; embarrassed, too, that he had written—jokingly to be sure—in 1919: "Will someone please send us a regiment or two of United States Marines?" But that was the accepted procedure for foreigners—missioners as well as business men—living in China at that time.

Warlords

It would have been difficult enough for a young missioner to establish the Church in Yeungkong even if the atmosphere had been peaceful. But the early years of Ford's mission career were hectic, hostile years. Scarcely a letter went back to Maryknoll without at least a passing reference to bandits or brigands or warlords. He worked and lived in a time and amid conditions which promised no security of living, no leisure for working out long-term plans.

The year before Francis Ford entered Maryknoll, the Manchu dynasty fell. Unfortunately for China there was no single force strong enough to replace it. Sun Yat-sen, the titular head of the revolution, had little or no influence over the revolutionaries. Governors and generals were more interested in preserving their personal domains than in the creation of a unified republic. Yüan Shih-kai, an able military leader, might have succeeded, but when he attempted to place himself on the imperial throne, the provinces revolted and Yüan was forced to abandon his plan. This set the stage for the disintegration of the entire country. The warlords took over. A warlord, so-called, might be a political or military official with enough following to terrorize the inhabitants and enforce his will. Until he was overthrown, he levied taxes and administered justice and just as frequently despoiled the countryside.

Much of the problem stemmed from the time-honored discrepancy between the standards of living of the literati-bureaucrats and the people. Officials resorted to illegal sources of income in order to maintain their status in a pre-determined standard of life. This was not necessarily a lust for extravagance; it was necessary to maintain one's place in the bureaucracy. The official's position was difficult to achieve and precarious to hold, dependent on the whim of a superior. The gifts an official would send to the head of his department were gifts squeezed from the common people.

The political unrest went on and Ford's letters to Maryknoll reflect his concern: ". . . a hundred soldiers reinforced our city wall," he reported, "while trenches again are dug flanking the approaches to the city." Later in the year more news of the fighting: "It's over two weeks since any kind of boat came to Yeungkong, so we are a bit hazy as to the nature of the present conflict . . . several thousand soldiers to the east of us have revolted and turned bandits . . . the hills about us are all dotted with soldiers and night patrols guard the city walls." Occasionally the mission property was invaded. Father Philip Taggart, Ford's assistant, wrote of one such incident: "A group of soldiers entered the mission, but at a word from Father Ford they left. Later in the night another group broke into the women's quarters; when they were leaving they fired three shots at Father Ford. . . ." Echoing St. Paul, Ford could, without exaggerating, say: "Our flesh had no rest, but we suffered all tribulation, combats without, fears within."

Imagine the uncertainty of the times, the distress of the poor people, fighting against eternal odds, helplessly caught in the struggle for existence. As always the poor suffered most. Preoccupied with the problem of pain and hunger, they cared little which warlord won; one was the same as the other. Bowed down by that most poignant, that most sorrowful of earthly conditions, injustice, they wanted only to be left in peace.

The poor maintained an essentially negative relationship to their officials even in normal times. They had no power to force the government to behave in an acceptable manner. People kept their distance, passively accepting their fate; the intolerable wrongs they would accept, but they would never admit defeat. With his deep concern for the people, Ford explained the situation this way in a letter sent in 1919 to Maryknoll: "Very often bona fide soldiers are not paid; they are sent out to collect their wages with good interest, by looting the common people. . . . No people in the world are so patient, or so desirous of being left alone, as these poor Chinese." Then with keen perception he predicted: "But they will not go on submitting indefinitely. There are those who fear that Bolshevism may find here an agreeable soil. The Christian foundation must be laid now; it will be difficult, if not impossible, to do so later on."

Love

The amazing point about Ford's early years in China was that, despite the political unrest and the hopelessly chaotic conditions, and despite the absence of directives from higher authority and the lack of a coordinated mission policy, he still managed to achieve a measure of success in his apostolic endeavors. Chief among the reasons was the emphasis he placed on preaching God's love—God was the solicitous Father of all. Ford would then try to show forth that divine love by *his* love for the Chinese. His buoyant, optimistic nature had much to do with his success; he refused to get discouraged, refused to concentrate on the overwhelming problems and obstacles. But more important than his cheerful outlook was his genuine high regard for the people: "There are positively no people," he wrote, "so lovable as the Chinese."

Ford wrote about the Catholic town crier ringing his bell and shouting: "Time for evening prayers. Come to night prayers." After a long arduous day in the fields, the handful of Christians would gather in one of their homes, or in the humble "chapel"—a rented shop on the side of the road, on the dirt floor of which was a simple wooden table altar. Behind the altar hung a faded picture of the Sacred Heart. The long distances they would walk to attend Mass on feast days touched Ford deeply, and made him more certain than ever that many more Chinese would appreciate the faith and the liturgy if only he could get the message to them.

Father Ford held his Chinese Christians in high admiration. The fact that they were an numerically insignificant minority did not lessen their fervor, nor his esteem. They were the part standing for the whole, incorporating the nation into the Mystical Body of Christ. To a certain extent the very fact of their being baptized into the Church separated the Chinese Christians from the majority of their fellow countrymen. Conversion to Christianity was regarded by many as an act of treason against the national way of life. Yet the last thing Ford wanted was a ghetto, an isolationist Christian community that required an enclosure in order to survive. He believed in pushing his fledgling Christians out of the nest; their strength and sincerity had to be tested. He looked upon his small groups of Christians as the leaven that would permeate and transform the whole area. He had a father's pride in them and loved to visit their villages. Sometimes he remained overnight in their dark, windowless homes, eating with the family, discussing the village problems with them, praying with them. After Mass and breakfast the next morning he would move on to the next village that had Christian families.

Agreeing with Pope Pius XI when he said the Chinese "tend naturally to solitude and prayers," Ford added, "The fact that it is a natural tendency does not make it the less enjoyable for us who work among them, and, granting these qualities, whenever you want a stimulant, just try to vision the world when China becomes Catholic."

Writing for the Maryknoll Mission magazine he contrasted the active liturgical participation of his Chinese Catholics with the "puritanic severity of American Catholic services which lays undue stress on external decorum and silence." In their own language, long before the Church's emphasis on the congregation's active role in the liturgy, the Chinese Christians chanted in unison not only their morning and evening prayers but all the common prayers of the Mass. The lay catechist would read the passages from the scripture and the priest would preach the word to the people.

In a characteristically light vein Ford described this lay participation.

This morning I tried to make my thanksgiving after Mass while the Christians prayed during the Mass that followed. Soon I found myself nursing a grudge against certain individuals in the congregation. With my eyes shut tight . . . I could still see the people behind the shouts that pierced my eardrums. An old man in the corner prays as though Heaven were as deaf as himself. A dear old lady in the back insists on chanting through her nose in a key that whines above them all; . . . our old gatekeeper chimes in strong on the "Our Father" whenever it occurs and subsides for the rest of the day. . . . One man answers the litany before the invocation has ended, his neighbor drawls out the "amen" long after the others have finished. These do be petty faults, no man's throat is musical so early in the morning, but still it calls for charitable thoughts to keep a calm mind in the midst of the tumult. This morning instead of trying to pray *against* them, I tried praying with them . . . and it made a difference; . . . the solemn hush at the Consecration showed these Christians could pray as well by silence as by noise and rebuked my carping criticism . . . ; but until such time as these zealous new Christians are disciplined to order and moderation, I am sure the good Lord will understand and accept their prayerful thanks.

These were simple people. The Yeungkong Christian community, with the exception of a few men returned from southeast Asia, was made up of the poor and the unsophisticated. No one was more conscious of their poverty than Ford himself. "It is too easy," he pointed out, "for the missioner to preach resignation to people who do not possess the means to buy food or clothing when he himself has a full belly and lacks nothing; . . . we are dealing with poor people, really poor people."

On the River

To care for his scattered flock the young missioner had to be on the road or, more accurately, on the water much of the time. Travel was slow, uncertain, and uncomfortable. But neither the delays nor the inconveniences seemed to annoy Father Ford. Throughout his life he refused to be disturbed by the trivialities of his daily routine, and he found a way to enjoy the slow pace of life. He wrote: "Squatting in the shade of a one-master sampan we actually spend whole days sailing poetically along as though time spent was eternity. I'm sure even a tramp would have qualms of conscience wasting so much time." Ford enjoyed every minute of it. "These sampans," he said, "are the squeamish landlubber's ideal in boats: no jerky puffing of a motor, no smell of smoky oil, they glide along rather like the motion of a canoe. . . . It lets a man think of other things besides his appetite."

Ford loved the rivers and the exotic sampans and high-pooped junks that plied them. He had the perfect temperament that permitted him to savor every new experience and to relax where others would become impatient and annoyed. He never complained of the slowness; he would watch for hours as the men and women, with a rythmic dance step, outer legs drawing back and forth with a ballet-like movement, their oars whipping the water like fins, performed nautical duties older than those of the Norsemen. The boat people were, it is true, an outcast group, illiterate but proud; a peaceful, industrious people who were born, lived, and died on their craft. The river and the sea were their world. In poetic mood after a long sampan trip Ford wrote: "A boat trip like this is the nearest I'll ever get to Nirvana! It hypnotizes thought and dulls the mind from dwelling on the curvatures of the body. It ends in a relaxation of all faculties, and the petty annoyances of days and dates and impending obligations are forgotten in the entire dedication of self to the supression of all desires. Impressions in such a state are wordless and without shape. . . . We are ready to grant (with the Chinese) that grace of motion lies in the absence of friction, hence the Oriental logically reasons that the greatest beauty lies in the total absence of friction . . . ; viewed thus our sampan trip is the perfection of poetry and beauty. . . ."

The leisurely pace, the effortless movement of the sampan soothed him. He would remove his shoes, squat on the floor of the boat, light his pipe, and wonder why the West loved speed. Nothing refreshed him more than the quiet hours of reading and prayer. "At night God is very near to us [on a Chinese sampan], and the plaintive cry, 'How shall we sing the song of the Lord in a strange land' is answered from the silence of our soul where God's work is near. And God consoles us in the absence of the Mass by making the sacrifice of it sweet, and instead of offering Him Himself we laugh at our empty hands and offer Him ourselves."

As the youthful pastor increased his journeys, his sensitive nature and keen power of observation discovered many virtues in the Chinese that he did not expect to find in a non-Christian people. Following a ride on a river boat he had this to say: "We whites pride ourselves on our democracy aboard ship; we chat with unknown deck companions and enjoy a freedom denied on land. Yet even in this the Chinese can give us pointers."

He recalled one day on board a junk when he travelled with a crowd of thirty simple, illiterate Chinese; from the moment he scrambled over the gunwhale until the boat docked the theme of the conversation was politely directed toward him. He was surprised that his companions knew so much about his work, about his orphanage, his school. They shared their meagre food and their water pipes with him. "You might say this is the usual Chinese form of politeness," he wrote, "which is true; but these men meant it. When we landed late that night, I intended to leave my baggage and send for it at dawn, but two of the sailors hoisted it on their shoulders and led the way to the mission. . . . Do you wonder our mission trips are so delightful?"

But as he sat near the door of his Yeungkong mission chapel he knew that the unsophisticated boatmen were the pleasant exception. In the town, panting in the 95° heat, where animated street stalls crowded the sidewalks and tireless urchins kicked unripe pomeloes with their bare feet, where itinerant peddlers hawked their wares, where restaurant tables—their black square surfaces overrun with great black flies—overflowed onto the street, where whiffs of grease and scents of spices mixed with the stench of stale urine, the disinterested hundreds still passed by. Here no doubt he thought of the sorrow of his Master: "All you who pass by the way, see if there be any sorrow like unto my sorrow." The heedless crowds seemed oblivious of the missioner who yearned to bring them the message of Christ. Sitting there, asking for strength to do God's will, Ford composed this quatrain:

> Cost what it may—to save one soul,
> Death or a lifelong toil for Thee—
> Gladly I offer all I can,
> Lord, in Thy goodness, strengthen me.

✿ CHAPTER III

JOHN C. H. WU

In the light of Christian Revelation I have come to
discover the scintillating stars of oriental mysticism
which should lead all peoples to the Fountain
of Life . . . to the joy of the Cross. . . . T'ao itself is
but a pointer to the Divine Logos.

INTERNATIONAL PHILOSOPHICAL QUARTERLY Feb. 1963

JESUS CHRIST

I am the way, and the truth, and the life.
No one comes to the Father but through me.

JOHN 14:6

The Early Years at Yeungkong

Francis Ford seemed most at home in the villages, with
their green rice fields and their gray mud-brick homes sur-
rounded by high broken walls, in the villages with their
twisting paths—all paths are twisted, for "the evil spirits
can travel only in straight lines—in the villages among the
simple, unhurried peasants, without remorse or dreams,
ignorant of the outside world. He would linger among the
toyless children with their noses running in the January
cold and their bodies sweating in the August sun. Here,
rather than in the noisy crowded market towns, he had

45

some success in adding to the Christianity left to him by the French Fathers.

For the most part these isolated pockets of Christianity, "islands in a huge sea of paganism," had their origin outside of China. Often the center of a Christian community was a Chinese business man returned from overseas where he had embraced Christianity, frequently through marriage with a Catholic woman. On returning to his native village with his wife and family, he kept the faith despite the non-Christian atmosphere of the village. Francis Ford added to the original believers slowly. A faithful chronicler, he recorded his efforts and reported them back to Maryknoll where his diaries were eagerly awaited. While he was tireless in caring for his scattered Christians, there is no question but that at this time he considered the gathering of new converts the principal object of his apostolate. He intended to build up the Church, convert by convert, to the point where its numerical strength would permit it to exert a Christian influence on the milieu. There was no thought yet of the importance of the Chinese national clergy, nor of the role the layman had in the mission of the Church. This was simply a foreign missionary priest-centered approach, assisted by Sisters and a few hired lay teachers of the doctrine.

His reports were generally cheerful, frequently humorous, always optimistic. "At Chashan there were twenty-five baptisms," he would write. Or, "Home again in Yeung-kong; the trip north gave us eighty-four confessions, six marriages, one hundred thirty-three baptisms. . . ." "Kolung . . . eight baptisms (one whole pagan family). Ten other men also were ready for baptism, but their wives were not, so we were obliged to put them off." Again, "I've fallen in love with Shek-kang, a purely Christian love of their fervor in studying the doctrine. . . . There are no Christians here, so there is no one to lower their zeal." He baptized forty-five in another village. "Not a large number," he conceded, but added, "I can truly say my arm was tired pouring the water."

Some of his journeying took him to offshore islands such as Chappo about which he wrote: "The first time I visited the island I wrote to you of its stainless sand, and simple souls, and fishing smacks and nets, and salted sea food. . . . My first impressions have been deepened . . . and my affection for the mainland is being weaned with each visit here." China for him was a land for dreaming as well as for hard work and hard thinking.

This early progress required funds to build small chapels in as many villages as possible. To the Christians of one village he promised a chapel as soon as they had enough converts to fill it. They soon gave him the congregation he asked for, as well as the ground he needed. Later they would give him the daily labor for the construction. What he wished to do here, he explained, was to build a chapel large enough for a congregation of two hundred, two classrooms for about seventy-five children, a bedroom on the end of the chapel for the priest or catechist, and a wall to surround it all. All this required money.

It pained him to ask for money from his friends back in America. He always apologized when he did so. "And please don't fear I'm thinking only of myself all the time," he wrote to Father James Anthony Walsh in 1923. "I've weighed the needs each time against the sufferings of millions in Austria, against the typhoon in Swatow, the famines in the north of China, the charity drives at home . . . and they quiet my longings and turn my prayers for you who are bearing the world's burdens. If I sometimes seem to confide my worries to you, it is simply to distract you from your own. Confidences in trouble are, you know, signs of dependence and friendship, for it isn't to everyone I would open up so loudly. However, let's call our problems 'hopes for the future.' . . ."

Still he knew there was money being used needlessly and foolishly back home. "The sum expended [on non-essentials] is staggering," he said, "and exasperating to a missioner in need of funds, and provocative of day dreams. Just suppose there were to be a cosmetic-less week, and the savings handed over to the missions. . . ." He knew this was wishful thinking, but occasionally someone reading his words would be moved to make a sacrifice of personal pleasure to send a gift for his work.

The early twenties were boisterous years in the Yeung-kong mission: warlords and bandits, periods of seige and brief intervals of peace, antiforeign demonstrations and anxious waiting for the next outburst. Once the mission was attacked by a mob. They broke down the outer door of the chapel, threw stones at the stained-glass windows, tore the holy pictures from the wall, and then assailed the rectory. Ford, describing the incident, wrote: "It was the narrowest escape I've had so far. If the stout door had not held, the mob would have been rough. It is a question if it would have been martyrdom, for though the motive expressed was hatred of the foreign religion, their real motive was a display of anti-Western sentiment and an itch to break things that all of us feel sometime in our youth."

On another occasion, Ford described his reactions when he encountered bandits in the Yeungkong area.

This was the first time I had met bandits. I was afraid, not of them, but of my lack of courage. When you want to impress your enemy by a stern frown or a gruff bearing, it is awkward to have your voice stutter or go up in a treble or to have the pipe in your mouth start to chatter. This is the first reaction to danger, it is physical and beyond the control of your will. Luckily, pride asserts itself; your knees grow firm and with the consciousness of being at ease, the humor of the situation strikes you. This could be just as bad, as you are tempted to grin at the bandits, which is not respectful.

Of course, you realize that ordinarily Chinese bandits do not lust for blood, but for money. If they find it necessary to hurt you, they will do so as gently as possible. There is only one chance in a hundred that you will suffer physical harm. . . .

My recent experience at sea was different. The bandits took the large steamer with its three hundred passengers and directed us out of our course for four days. This was not mere child's play; not the impulsive act of hungry men along the side of the road. This had been carefully planned and meant death in case of failure; so the pirates were in dead earnest.

In the midst of these problems, Ford received a welcome boon. Maryknoll Sisters were anxious to begin their work, and it was to the Yeungkong mission that the first group was sent in 1921. Ford met them at the dock with a large group of Christians equipped with a band and the traditional fireworks.

A few months later, the pastor wrote back to Maryknoll:

I am only now beginning to realize what changes the Sisters' presence will make. Take the orphanage, for example: under our benign and benighted regime the place was an eyesore. . . . Since the Sisters have taken charge the babies cry whenever they are hungry, for they know it is the prearranged signal for feeding. In my time they gave up crying in disgust, as it brought no results. I knew nothing about a baby's formula and less about preparing it. The seminary course, except for a tract on infant baptism, never touched on babies. Now, perhaps for the first time in their wee lives, they are washed in warm water and dusted with powder and they smile in their dreams.

The Sisters did not send as many infants to heaven as he did, he jokingly remarked, for the babies decided to enjoy life.

Although the Sisters knew they were working with an understanding and appreciative superior, Ford found it difficult to praise the Sisters to their faces. He seldom spoke words of praise directly to his missioners. Once, after telling one of his priests, "It is surprising to me how you manage to get so much done," he quickly added: "Of course, I don't want you to sit back now and congratulate yourself! It's probably the reason I'm so chary of praise—in my own case it goes to my head, or at least to my feet, and justifies an immediate rest."

Ford, however, had no hesitation in extolling the Sisters in his letters to Maryknoll. He wrote:

I have been rather silent about the Sisters at Yeung-kong and have been trying to analyze just why. I think it is because they are as much Maryknoll as we men are and praising them would be akin to lauding ourselves. Then again, the work the Sisters do is not spectacular, and so regularly efficient is it that we are not thrilled by it. You, however, at Maryknoll who have depended so much on the Sisters from the start can appreciate what their presence means to Yeungkong. It may seem like a rash statement, but I think it is true that there is very little future for any mission that has not Sisters working there.

During these early years in Yeungkong, Father Ford continued to observe, to study, and to plan. He had no illusions about the difficulties of his mission. Bringing into being fundamental institutions such as seminaries, novitiates, and schools is a slow, laborious process. How could he adapt the Western-orientated religion to the mentality and needs of an Eastern people with deep-seated traditions and an ancient culture? How could he make the message powerful enough, distinctive enough, and relevant? The Church as he saw it was but nibbling at the edges of the problem. The dimensions of the missioner's task were vast, challenging, and staggeringly complex. Vision and daring were needed, but above all understanding and knowledge of the people among whom he lived.

All Gods Equally Honored

For a Chinese to become a Christian, even for the poorest of them, was a wrenching, violent ordeal. The fact that they were joining a religion that seemed to be coming from the West did not make the conversion any easier. The missioner had to understand that he did not go to a people without religion. The Chinese on the whole were religious. It would be difficult, however, and perhaps inaccurate, as Francis L. K. Hsu admits in his *Americans and Chinese*, to describe the individual Chinese as a Buddhist, or a Taoist, or a Confucianist, or an ancestor worshiper. An American might say he was a Jew or a Protestant or a Catholic; a Chinese would be hard put to say exactly what he was.

Lou Tseng-Tsiang, even after he became a Benedictine monk, said many times "I am still a Confucianist." A person in the West belongs to a Church. At least the vast majority does. And normally an American believes that his is the true Church, and he wishes that Church to prevail over all others.

In China it was quite different. A Chinese may go to a Buddhist shrine one day seeking some favor and to a Taoist temple another time for something else, for each temple is dedicated to special gods who have influence in specific spheres. The temple interiors may be hideous in their darkness, sheltering bats and screeching rats; they may repel with the scent of stale incense, but their gods are there for practical purposes; one to stop a flood, one to produce rain, another to halt an epidemic, or to help in a business venture. Once the end is served, the Chinese have no further need of the god until the next emergency. In some Chinese temples one might find statues of Buddha, Confucius, and Lao Tzu equally prominent. During World War II, GI's were amazed to find, on occasion, Christ and Mohammed displayed on the same altar with the Chinese gods.

The Chinese felt that all gods must be equally honored —certainly none should be overlooked, nor should one ever be an object of contempt; but there was seldom any personal or emotional attachment to these gods.

Although Ford considered Christianity the absolute religion determined for all mankind, still he would not say there was no truth or goodness in, for example, Buddhism; nor would he attempt to attack what he considered error in it. He thus avoided embarrassment and irritation. He would preach the truth as he perceived it, but without attacking errors. Still, he grieved that it was Buddhism and not the gospel that had entered China at the beginning of the Christian era.

The missioner who had neither the time nor the inclination to delve into the intricacies of Chinese religious thinking would, of course, find the Chinese attitude toward the realm of spirits quite unintelligible. To be successful, Frank Ford and all missioners were forced to appreciate the fact that the Chinese world of spirits was essentially similar to their world of human beings. The Chinese structure in both worlds functioned in a similiar manner. As a man on earth would be judged, so the souls of the deceased were reviewed by a hierarchy of officials. Those who were found guilty of evil during their life on earth were condemned to various types of punishment; those who were without sin were given various degrees of reward. Obviously the ordinary Chinese had a strong belief in a life after death and a belief that he would be held accountable for the actions he performed on earth.

As he made his visits to non-Christian homes, Ford found the most common idol was the kitchen god. The kitchen god and his wife were believed to ascend to heaven on the seventh day before the Chinese New Year to report on the conduct of the family during the past year. On that day most families would make an offering before the household altar dedicated to the pair. The offerings pleased the deities and assured the family that the report taken to heaven would be favorable.

Because the Chinese had no personal intimate association with their gods, they frequently resorted to divination. This was a serious obstacle to the Christian missioner and a great temptation to new converts. There was hardly a town or village of any size that did not have its diviners and fortune-tellers, who were consulted on every conceivable matter: the best day and hour to start plowing, the propitious hour to start a journey, the ideal place to build a home or dig a grave, whom to marry, and what type of business to pursue.

The Chinese believed that their sufferings on earth could have been caused by the sins of their deceased parents, or their grandparents. Their happiness and wealth on the other hand could have been the result of the exemplary conduct of their parents or ancestors in a previous existence. With this in mind, it is easier to understand why ancestor worship was so fundamental to all Chinese religious belief, and why it was so widely practiced among the Chinese. This worship of ancestors is in no way analogous to the Westerner's pride in his genealogy. The cult in China was quite different, and except for Chinese Christians and Mohammedans, all Chinese adhered to this practice. It was literally the "universal religion of China," even though the people would simultaneously have faith in Buddha or Confucius or the T'ao. Ancestor worship, needing no vast temples or elaborate ritual, was the link between the Chinese world of humans and their world of spirits. It gave meaning and direction to all their other religious acts and doctrines; it was the active ingredient in every aspect of Chinese life. The ritual was explained in this manner: (1) All living persons owe their fortune or misfortune to their ancestors; misfortune is an evidence of one's ancestors' evil life; good fortune is a proof of one's ancestor's virtuous life. (2) The departed ancestors, like human beings on earth, have many needs, so food and paper images of clothing, furniture, and servants were offered in order that the departed might set up a comfortable home in the spirit world. (In recent times even paper automobiles have been offered at a grave.)

A knowledge of the ancestor rite was necessary to an

understanding of why a Chinese who died without male offspring was an object of public pity, why he was doomed forever to be a "spiritual tramp" with no one to supply his needs. It also explains why normally an only son of a Chinese Christian family did not aspire to the celibate priesthood, though there were notable exceptions. The worst imaginable plight for any Chinese was, while alive, to be without known parents and relatives, and, when dead, to be without living descendants.

The Christian missioner who held a firm belief in one omnipotent God had to make it clear in his dealings with Chinese that he regarded their gods as idols and the worshiper guilty of idolatry. The Chinese liked the idea of having many gods. To be told that when they accepted the God of Christianity they must abandon all other gods seemed unreasonable to them. In their minds there did not seem to be a question of which gods are true and which false—any or all might be true.

As Father Ford studied the religious background of the Chinese, he realized the great obstacles the Church faced in attempting to change the religious habits of the people and to convert them to the one true God. He knew that not by learned talk nor human industry was he going to convert them, nor could he save them "through dialectics," as St. Ambrose had said. It would be through the "simplicity of faith" about which Paul speaks in Corinthians. Patience was required; a people immersed in the beliefs of a lifetime must be approached very slowly. Ford saw that understanding and love were also required on the part of the missioner if he was to make any progress. "We may easily fall into the error," he wrote in the mid-twenties, "of thinking that the prejudice is all on the part of the Chinese people. We often take the attitude that the difficulties are all one-sided. How often do we begin a statement with: 'the trouble with China is,' without much thought that we ourselves might be that cause. . . ." With deep sympathy he said: "Let us hope that in converting them we shall not make them irreverent of agelong beauty, iconoclasts of aught but pagan idols." Buddha, for Ford, could be in a sense a great precursor of Christ.

In 1923 he wrote: "Perhaps . . . I had aimed too low in estimating the Chinese so that every additional evidence of virtue is refreshing and I want to shout it from the housetops . . . for every wholesale commendation that escapes me, I have choked down and stifled hundreds just as laudatory. . . . I have been hoping that someone with less care for public opinion would openly state the thesis that the Chinese are naturally the most advanced race on earth. . . . I am sick of posing as a superior white man in the face of contrary evidence."

As Ford saw it, one of the main causes of China's resentment against the West was the Westerners' arrogant assumption that the "white fathers"—and this applied to some missioners as well as to Western diplomats and business people—knew what was best for the backward people of Asia and that the decisions of the man from the West must be accepted whether or not the Asians liked them.

He knew instinctively that an overbearing attitude would never be palatable to the people of China. While Westerners had faults with which the Chinese were well acquainted, the Chinese had virtues about which the ordinary American knew nothing.

In 1925 Ford answered a letter from Father Walsh: "Yes, I have been reluctant to write about the situation here simply because it is primarily not religious but political. Certainly in our area it is not as exciting now as the U.S.

press would make you think. And I suspect we know as much about what's going on as other foreigners, especially the old-fashioned type who have been used to looking on the Chinese somewhat as though they were created to serve the white man." This was a sore point with Francis Ford and he returned to it again and again. In his letter to Father Walsh he admitted: "Perhaps I am a bit too sensitive on this point and too unjust in undervaluing the white man's civilization, but it is easy to become a cynic when asked to stomach the arguments offered."

He went on to explain the effects of the United States news features on the bandits in China. "This leads to bitterness and a lack of objectivity in reporting the news; for the Chinese press then responds by featuring United States murders, rapes and robberies." He pictured the foreign press coming suddenly face to face with the Chinese dragon and, because of little or no orientation or preparation for the assignment, reporters "mistake the dragon's normal breathing for violent agitation." Ford admitted that there were serious problems in China's political and economic life; no doubt he underestimated their gravity when he referred to these disturbances as "her periods of St. Vitus' dance." He cautioned the correspondents not to get "hysterical if China still twitches now and then." "Old Grandmother Europe," he added with strong irony, "slightly nearsighted, almost smothered China in the swaddling bands of 'spheres of influence,' fed her soothing narcotics instead of the milk of human kindness." Now Europe seems horrified, he added, "to find the child alive and kicking"—and considerably more than a child in the world of complex political maneuvering.

Ford knew that it was in the very nature of all men to value and love their own country and its traditions. Therefore, he was constantly concerned about the most effective way to introduce to the Chinese people the teachings of Christ without giving them cause for repulsion or resentment. It would be necessary, of course, to effect certain changes in the ancient customs proper to China, but he was convinced these changes should be as few as possible and only gradually introduced. In this matter Frank Ford seemed to be far more liberal than were most of the European bishops, and most of the Chinese bishops too, who associated China's relative political and economic weakness with her pagan past. The Chinese clergy had been trained in the Western tradition—many of them having studied in Rome—and they felt that progress was to be found in breaking completely with the past in all things, and moving into a Western type future, free from the trappings of superstition and idolatry.

But the tradition runs deep in China and age-old customs are not easily abandoned. The long New Year celebration was an example. It was a time for universal rejoicing. The crops were in, it was a leisure season, a time for family reunions, with meat and wine at the meals. For the missioner, however, it could be a very lonely period, the one time of year when he was especially out of touch with the common sentiment. And for many fervent native Christians also it could be a difficult period.

Ford tried desperately to understand the aspirations of the Chinese. He would defend their culture and he wanted all missioners to respect their traditions. Rather bitterly he wrote on one occasion: "We must love before we can truly value an alien culture. Ignorance . . . is not the only explanation of racial antipathies, antipathies arise from indifference; all alien cultures are prejudged outlandish and even inexplicable. . . . When from the outset judgments are jaundiced by antipathy or indifference, continued residence simply entrenches the prejudices." He caustically blamed much of the misunderstanding about the Chinese to foreign traders who seldom ventured beyond the port cities; or on the unreliable anecdotes of passing travelers: their generalities, he said, have gradually seeped into the Westerner's concept of the Oriental, until it has become "almost axiomatic that the Asiatic is odd, exotic, deviously cunning, and impenetrably different from the rest of men—a person who will do anything to save face. As though face-saving is a sacred monopoly of the Oriental." At the dinner table once he said if he were a Chinese, he would be appalled by the curious web of facts and fancies the foreigner had woven concerning him; to say nothing of the disparaging remarks about him carried in the Western press.

When he became Bishop, Ford would allow none of his missioners to scoff at the religion or the morals of the Chinese. They were to be genuinely sympathetic and responsive toward the human values they encountered. He reminded the priests in his charge that they had come to China not only to impart Christianity to the people, but to receive something from their culture and history.

Maryknoll's first student had a deep understanding of human nature. He understood its irritability, sensitiveness, changeableness, blindness. He also knew its charity, its humility, and its beauty. He knew his own feelings and failings, and his empathic mind made him intimately aware of the feelings and the virtues as well as the failings of the Chinese people.

The Role of the Missioner

In Francis Ford's mind there was never a thought that his missionary vocation was something extraordinary, something heroic. Christ had commanded his followers "Go into the whole world and preach the gospel." This, as far as Ford was concerned, was the task God called him to. The Church in China had allowed itself to become linked with dominant Western political and economic forces. Ford came to realize how unfortunate it was that the missionary effort of the past century coincided chronologically with the colonial expansion of Europe. And even so, despite the backing of the Western powers, the Church had not been able to give the Chinese the gospel message. Ford felt that he was chosen to go and teach the doctrine and to help establish the Church in China.

About five years after he reached China, Ford wrote an article about the "lure of the missions":

> The Church's long years of experience and experiment give confidence to the apprentice missioner so that he is willing confidently to sign on for life and identify himself with a cross. The success of the Church's enterprise in new fields depends on the assurance that her personnel will carry on in normal obedience. . . . This is the missioner's real test of courage and enthusiasm. If the missioner . . . is to venture into strange circumstances, he must be content with the restraints of teamwork and steady monotony; the sea to be charted is new, but the routine is without glamor. Frequently the unseen horizon is forgotten in the tedium of the nearest wave, and the hand becomes calloused and the eye weary keeping the wheel pointed with the compass.
>
> To be successful then, must a missioner be a mere automaton? . . . No, a thousand times!

Ford knew the Orient could be a land of exciting adventure to a heart aflame with the zest to woo it, or dismally silent and cold when the echo of God's voice was spent. Seen at a distance, the lands of the East were a challenge to be met for Christ; often this perspective was lost in the dust and glare of the relentless sun; the stamina to achieve was weakened as the task loomed gigantic in the terrible heat.

Ford emphasized that the "one test of success" in the Orient was the missioner's willingness to take whatever comes in weather fair or foul. "The local conditions beyond the missioner's control," he said, "do not alter the contract and his success is gauged under such difficulties by his perseverance, not by measures to avoid them—resolving itself into 'monotonous fidelity' as is the case of priests everywhere."

The motive that would strengthen and sustain the will "through the humdrum dog-days of the tropics," he pointed out was "that of sharing in the obedience of Christ." The basic attractiveness of mission life lay essentially in its "opportunity to share in the work of redemption," which he repeated was common to the Church's mission everywhere. The work in pagan lands he believed "in its essence differs not at all from apostolic work in any other land."

There was, in Ford's thinking, even at this early stage of his mission career, substantially very little difference between the work of a priest in New York, or New Mexico, and the work of the foreign missioner in China. "Mission work in China," he wrote, "is run along lines very similar to work at home . . . There is work here for the most ardent character and there is still more work aplenty for us poor mortals of a coarser mold, and it is this daily routine work that is unheralded in the annals of the missions."

Later, as he matured, Father Ford closely approached the insights of Vatican II on mission in the Church. He wrote: "If Americans were to realize that mission work is the ordinary, normal life of the Church, our seminaries could not contain the applicants . . . If mission life is the normal life of the Church, then it cannot make demands that are impossible of human nature: if it is the very life of the Church, then it is not enough that a scattered few offer themselves."

It became his conviction that the qualities needed for a foreign mission vocation were practically the same as those required for any priest. In addition to the ordinary Christian virtues, the missioner in a pagan country should be well supplied with "cheerfulness in adverse conditions," and have the "power of accommodation." Next Ford would emphasize physical fitness, which he thought of as an ability to endure, rather than strength of body. He looked for convictions rather than skills. The capacity to philosophize over the excessively humid heat and the biting damp cold, to be patient in the trying travel conditions, to be content with the lack of ordinary comforts and conveniences— these he thought of more value than mere good health.

Ford thought it essential for a missioner to have "the spirit of study more than mere knowledge." The best missioner, he felt, was the man who appreciates his own limitations—in the language, for example—and continues to study even after many years in another land; the man who knows he does not possess all the knowledge of theology and Scripture and is anxious to develop himself in these sciences. The missioner should have more than the average taste for reading, Ford thought, and should possess a humble, inquiring attitude, else much of the native philosophy will escape him. "Mission work," he said, "is being carried on more and more among civilized people who are improving themselves daily through education . . . and the missioner must be equipped accordingly." As a guilding principle, he suggested that the missioners be "primarily spiritual leaders sent to save souls and only secondarily social reformers."

"Spiritually," he said, "the missioner should be grounded in humility . . . in the obligation of prayer . . . and in the spirit of persevering self-sacrifice." Over and above the qualities and virtues of every priest, he said the foreign missioner must have those dispositions that will help him to carry on when alone. A missioner in a pagan land is "thrown for mere companionship more into his own communing with God. In crowded alleys, on mountain trails, on sampan trips, he must bring his God with him in his thoughts. . . ."

Francis Ford thought one of the most serious vices of the missioner was condescension, defined as "the act of being gracious, affable as with an inferior." Some men seem to think of this as a virtue: certainly he did not. "Our Lord never condescended," he said. "He emptied Himself and took the form of a man; Christ never betrayed superiority in His dealing with others." Ford pointed out that the missioner may be better educated in the sciences and arts than most of his people and he may have enjoyed a higher standard of living; but this did not entitle the missioner to "set himself apart as an expert, not only in the things that pertain to God, but also in everything else." In 1932, he wrote:

> The Catholic Church, when she sends out her missioners to pagan lands, is not directly interested in the material welfare of the natives. She does not expect her apostles to become explorers or scientists, doctors or educators. She does not ask them to civilize the savage or to Westernize the Oriental. The missioner

to China does not go with a Bible in one hand and a mop in the other to "brighten some little corner" of the world. Dirt and disease and antiquated living habits and inefficiency in business methods are not his special concern. He does not lament the fact that English is not spoken, that there is no radio in every room, or that the people have never heard of halitosis.

Francis Ford seemed to regard with a bit of suspicion those missioners who were intent on the civilizing effects of Christianity. Christ, in his mind, came to save the world, not to civilize it. Certainly he was not obsessed with the idea of technical progress. His goal was not to make the Chinese prosperous except through moral values and spiritual influences. He preferred to raise their spirit of self-sacrifice and brotherhood than their standard of living. He repeated in 1945 what he had said in 1926: "Our task is to establish as complete a Church as possible." This was his strategy— confront the people head on with the message of the gospel, as he believed the apostles did in the early years of the Church.

Looking back now at the mission methods of the '30's and '40's it is easy for us to see defects and shortcomings. In order to make the Church relevant would it have been more cogent to think of the region as a corporate whole rather than to concentrate on isolated individuals within the region? Would it have been more effective to have given the people, in their Chinese environment, more guidance as to their social responsibilities in a revolutionary situation? By involving themselves in social problems the missioners might have made it apparent that Christianity could help the people more than could Communism.

But in the thirties and forties the social mission of the

Church had not been developed nor assimilated to the level of Pope John XXIII's encyclical "*Mater et Magistra*." There was little direction from Rome and there was little or no communication with the other bishops of China. There was no sign then of the collegiality of the bishops about which Vatican Council II was to speak at such great length. Travel was difficult and each bishop had his own responsibility walled off by a geographical boundary.

Ford tried to find the answer to this one question: What was to be done here and now to build up a Christianity among a people who were indifferent to the gospel message? By and large, he had to work out his own system.

Always for Ford there was but the one priesthood: preaching, consoling, leading, administering. "The Sacraments must be administered," he wrote, "and though the setting is different over here, the essentials remain the same. The relative poverty and uncouthness of pagan surroundings indeed distract and dampen enthusiasm rather than quicken it. In the abstract it would seem thrilling to bring Viaticum over steep mountain paths to a distant village. The fact is, however, the inconvenience of heat and weariness, the incongruous squalor of a village hut, and the pagan neglect of sick neighbors rob the scene of any poetry. The poetry is there, of course, if seen by faith, but the beauty is all within . . . and it strikes the missioner according to his viewpoint."

Always he returned to the importance for the missioner of knowledge and understanding of things Chinese. As early as 1920, when he was beginning to learn something of the Chinese people and their traditions, he wrote in a letter to the seminarians at Maryknoll: "The priest has a view of the Chinese that is often not that of the Europeans of the port cities. Perhaps love is the bridge. . . ."

Always it was his unshakeable belief that the role of the missioner was not "to convince the Asiatic that the western form of government and the western taste in art, or architecture, or mechanics are preferable to the native style."

In an article written in 1932, twenty years before his imprisonment and death, Ford expressed very clearly the basic reason for his ultimate rejection by the country he loved so dearly. "How often," he observed, "the accusation has been brought against the missioner by the oriental that he is the advance agent of Western imperialism. Too often the Cross in the hand of the missioner has been quickly followed by the battleships or exploiting trading companies of the West, and the two have been so linked as to be inseparable. . . ." Ford repudiated the association, but he knew, despite his writings to the contrary, that in the minds of many Chinese, particularly the teachers and students, the connection seemed to be unmistakable. How, in the natural order, could one explain to a non-Christian Chinese the missioner's presence among them? The majority found it difficult to distinguish between the missioner's objectives and the objectives of the Western country from which he came.

 # CHAPTER IV

CHUANG TZU

*Perfect love is the Queen of all virtues. Filial piety,
fraternal love, justice and loyalty are its handmaids.*
THE BOOK OF CHUANG TZU Ch. 14, p. 80

SAINT PAUL

*Love is patient, is kind; love does not envy,
is not pretentious, is not puffed up, is not ambitious,
is not self-seeking, is not provoked; . . . bears
with all things, believes all things, hopes all things,
endures all things.*
I CORINTHIANS 13:4–7

Kaying

After Father Thomas Frederick Price's death, Father James E. Walsh was appointed mission superior and in 1927 he became the first bishop of the Kongmoon mission of which the Yeungkong area was a part. Father Bernard Meyer, the third member of the pioneer group, had begun work in 1925 in Kwangsi Province. (He later became the first superior of the Prefecture of Wuchow.)

In the summer of 1925, the Congregation for the Propogation of the Faith assigned a new mission territory to Maryknoll. The Paris Foreign Mission Society priests of the Swatow vicariate felt that because of their limited personnel they could no longer adequately cover their vast mission field, so they petitioned Rome to divide the territory. The logical Maryknoller to direct the new mission was thirty-three year old Francis Ford, still boyish in appearance, but a missioner mature beyond his years, possessing an enviable wealth of experience.

Ford was accompanied by Father James Drought when he departed from his beloved Yeungkong. They left Hong Kong aboard the overnight coastal steamer headed north to Swatow. Father Raymond A. Lane, later to be appointed bishop in a new territory in Manchuria, was at that time Maryknoll's procurator in Hong Kong. Recalling Fathers Ford and Drought as they departed for the new territory, he wrote, "Rarely have I seen anyone so filled with joyful, vivacious interest. . . . They had the lightest equipment imaginable, hardly more than one would take for a day's picnic."

After spending a day with the hospitable Paris Foreign Missioners in Swatow, the two Maryknollers boarded a train for Chao Chow Fu. From there they took a river boat to Tsung Kow, and then covered the final thirty miles of the two hundred and fifty mile journey on foot.

The territory for which Ford was to be responsible lay between the twenty-third and twenty-fifth degrees of north latitude, in the northeast corner of Kwangtung province. It bordered on the German Dominican Fathers' mission in Fukien and the American Vincentians' mission in Kiangsi. In size the new mission was about equal to the states of Massachusetts, New Hampshire, and Vermont. The population of about three and a half million was scattered in seventy-eight market towns and innumerable villages throughout the extremely mountainous area.

On all modern maps of China the See city of the new mission is designated *Meihsien*, but habitually Ford and all Maryknollers used its ancient name, *Kaying*. The day after his arrival there, Ford sent the following message back to Maryknoll: "We enter our new field blessed in many ways and we are grateful for our blessings." But, as he realistically viewed the area and the small percentage of Christians, he added, "the work before us is vast and challenging . . . but we are young and . . . willing to work with all our strength for the conversion of this mission given to us by Rome to evangelize."

One problem loomed large and immediate—communication. In his Yeungkong mission, Ford had lived with people who spoke the Cantonese dialect. Without linguistic training or textbooks, he had learned the language sufficiently well. But he acquired his Chinese—"that outlandish tongue," as he called it—with difficulty and only by diligent application to the task. Now, after seven years of Cantonese, he had to learn the Hak-ka dialect, which is as different in sound from Cantonese as French is from German.

Ford never learned to speak the Hak-ka language with any degree of accuracy. He had no trouble understanding what was spoken to him, but at times his Hak-ka listeners found it difficult to follow him. His Cantonese background was always betraying itself.

Ford often felt the disadvantage of his verbal clumsiness. He wrote that "the three priests who were here previously were Chinese, and my halting tongue contrasts unfavorably with their fluency. The French priest who built up this mission was also a distinguished linguist, the compiler of two Chinese-French dictionaries of this Hak-ka dialect; so it is a new experience for these people to meet someone who cannot speak their language well."

With the help of a Chinese scholar, Father James Drought compiled a Hak-ka-English grammar and dictionary. By no means a definitive textbook, it was a creditable piece of work and served the early missioners fairly well.

The Hak-kas

Father Ford frequently referred to Maryknoll's new territory as the "Hak-ka Mission," rather than the Kaying mission. He wanted to distinguish it from the Cantonese- and Mandarin-speaking missions in Kongmoon and Wuchow. As he pointed out, the name Hak-ka was specific to his area, for the Hak-ka people were pretty much confined within the limits of the new mission.

The term Hak-ka is the romanized form for the Chinese characters meaning guest family or traveling family. The Chinese who were dwelling in Kwangtung province when the strangers from the north migrated into the territory gave them the name. Three centuries before Christ the Hak-ka people were living in the northern provinces of Shantung and Shansi. They were a peaceful tribe, flourishing in the fruitful, fertile land between the Yellow River and the Great Wall. As the population increased there was not enough land for everyone, so the Hak-kas had to yield and move on. During the Chin period they were forced to migrate south to the provinces of Honan and Anhwei, where they dwelt for about six hundred years. The Tsin Dynasty revolution (circa 419 A.D.) forced them to move again still farther south to the mountainous reaches of Kiangsi and Fukien. Two hundred years later, a new revolution pushed them into the chain of mountains which lie between Kiangsi and Kwangtung. They attempted to settle along the Kwangtung coastal region, but again were forced to move. Finally they arrived at the city of Kaying which they made their headquarters. Even then they had to fight frequently for existence. The final and most brutal conflict took place against the Cantonese in the year 1865. In this civil war thousands of Hak-kas were killed. This costly strife forced the weakened remnants to retreat into the inhospitable mountainous area of the province where Ford found them in 1925.

For the readers of Maryknoll's mission magazine, Ford gave this brief account of his people: "The Hak-ka Chinese should be of special interest to Americans because their history finds its echo in the lives of our own parents or grandparents. One incident in their history, their migration from the north down the hundreds of miles of Middle China to the tropical zone, also parallels the exodus of the Chosen People under Moses from Egypt to Palestine, or the enforced migration of the Arcadians from the bleak shores of Canada to our milder climate, or under somewhat different circumstances, it may be likened to the immigration of the smaller groups from Ireland, Germany and other European countries to the more friendly shores of America. . . . The Hak-kas of today are a living picture of our own forefathers in America . . . and as such they merit our special study."

Ford observed that the Hak-kas had many of the good characteristics of frontier people: a readiness to help one another, an ability to be satisfied with nature's harshest moods, a love of home that suffering in common begets, and a strict code of morals.

The Maryknoller from Brooklyn often referred to the Hak-ka people as his "kith and kin," and he admitted that he was prejudiced in their favor. Although he found them "superstitious," they were "gracious, hospitable people, scrupulous in the cult of ancestor worship."

He compared the Hak-kas not only to the pioneer

American settlers; they were also like the simple peasants of Biblical times. "Once we have penetrated into the interior of China," he observed, "we are struck by its 'oriental' atmosphere—not only oriental in the modern sense of exotic, luxuriant, languorous sensuality, but the orient of our Lord's time. A land devoted to simple agriculture, with a barefoot people who walk, not ride, who bear the heat of the day and the burden, who gather crops by hand and winnow the chaff in the wind, who draw water from the pool, who make bricks with mud and straw and burn the grass of the field for fuel: a land whose temples have porticoes and whose cities are girt with walls, whose blind and lame sit begging at the city gate and whose lepers are a common sight . . . where fishermen let down their nets, where fishing boats are tossed by typhoons; where the sower goes down to sow his seed; where in a word, the simple life, uncontaminated by modern inventions is still preserved."

The Hak-ka farmers had a hard life but they were clever; they belonged to the soil. There was no such thing as a tractor. No one had the money to buy one, and even if he did, the paddies were too small for tractors. They plowed with a water buffalo. The families that didn't own a buffalo either rented one or plowed by hand. Ordinarily they grew two crops of rice in the area, and after the second harvest in November they might try a few fields of winter wheat. They also planted sweet potatoes—the poor man's food—which grew well in the sandy soil, and peanuts which produced oil and a cash crop. The vines of the sweet potatoes and peanuts were dried and chopped up for food for the pigs and water buffalo—if the family was fortunate enough to own a buffalo.

Ford made it clear that the migration of the Hak-kas

from Shantung in the north was "purely for peace, for the right to till the soil, for the right to live. . . ." Continually pressed on to less fruitful soil, they were obliged to subsist on the rocky hillsides, unclaimed by others as worthless ground. Groups of Hak-kas moved into neighboring provinces, but for the most part they confined themselves to the area that has Kaying as its center. That is, those who remained in China confined themselves to this area; but the Hak-ka is a traveler and he is to be found in almost every large city of the world.

As they became more numerous, the Hak-kas found it extremely difficult to support their families; so through the years thousands and thousands of Hak-kas emigrated to Taiwan, Singapore, Borneo, Saigon, Bangkok, and the islands of the Pacific, where they quickly became a powerful business element. The Hak-kas had little difficulty outworking and outselling the inhabitants of the countries in the south, and many of them prospered. When they had accumulated enough money they returned to their homes in the Hak-ka hills, frequently bringing with them a wife and family.

So many men emigrated from the area that it resulted in a scarcity of male labor. Consequently, among the Hak-kas the women have customarily engaged in the heaviest type of manual work; cultivating the fields, carrying heavy burdens on their strong shoulders, walking long distances on big, strong feet. It is very likely that the Hak-kas left their Shantung homes before the bizarre custom of binding the feet of women became the vogue. At any rate the Hak-ka women always abhorred the custom and steadfastly refused to follow the otherwise universally practiced tradition. Ford jokingly referred to his territory as "a man's paradise, because the women do all the work."

Ford had high hopes for his people, particularly for the young men whom he hoped would remain at home to develop the region. He looked forward to the day when the area would have its own industries to keep the families together. "Inevitably and soon," he optimistically wrote a year after his arrival in Kaying, "these coal fields will be mined and emigration will stop from lack of motive to move on. This region, so close to the seaports of Swatow, Canton, and Hong Kong is bound to become an important manufacturing center, and the Hak-kas will possess the land. . . . Incidentally," he added, compensating himself for the loss of so many fine young men, "their experience in foreign ports will stand them in good stead when they return here. Then, and not until then, can we sit back and drop our worries over emigration and *its* evils, to begin a study of industrial crimes and *their* solutions."

On the other hand, Ford pointed out in an article in Maryknoll's mission magazine, "This emigration has had at least one beneficial result. The Hak-kas journeying to Siam and Singapore, and especially to Mauritius, found strong Catholic communities already established, and, on their return to China, many brought with them this new faith and frequently their Catholic wives. . . . As a matter of history the Catholic religion was first introduced into this region, not by missioners, but by the people themselves. . . . In the 1850's, native Hak-kas returning from the South Seas begged the bishop of Canton to send missioners to their villages, where they had already prepared the way among their relatives. . . ."

The missioners of the Paris Foreign Mission Society had labored in the Hak-ka territory since 1849. For the first decade—or until the Western powers had concluded the treaty with China that guaranteed all foreigners safety and all missioners freedom to preach—the priests had to keep in hiding most of the time because of the bitter anti-foreign and anti-Christian feeling that existed.

The French priests were faithful chroniclers and they recorded the details of the introduction of Christianity into the Hak-ka region. Père Hervel's diary gives the following details: "A young man named Hung-Tong had gone to Siam and thence to Penang to seek his fortune. There he heard about the Christian doctrine. He believed and embraced the religion of the Lord of Heaven in 1844. Returning to his native village of Shou-Hang, about fifteen miles from Kaying, he brought the faith to some of his relatives. Hung-Tong continued his efforts to win others to Christ and in a few years he had many believers around him who asked for a priest to come and baptize them. Their desire was soon fulfilled. Father Le Turdu . . . came to Kaying early in 1850." As far as is known he was the first Christian missioner to reach the city. But the followers of the Prince of Peace were given little understanding and less peace by their neighbors who looked upon the Christians as a part of the imperialistic West.

In 1851, the Christians of Shou-Hang were falsely accused of crimes against the State and soldiers were sent to burn the little chapel and to arrest Father Le Turdu. The head of the village and the priest were imprisoned in Kaying where the former became critically ill and died a few days after his release.

The Hak-ka Christians suffered continually during those early years. Chapels were desecrated, Christian families were harassed, young men known to be Catholic were refused opportunities for political or educational advancement. However, in the year 1885, after a strong warning from the French government, the Kaying mandarin gave Père

Hervel authorization to retake possession of the chapels and oratories in the district. For the next several decades, under the direction of the energetic French Fathers and with no serious persecution of the Church, the sprawling Hak-ka mission made fairly substantial gains in the number of its Christians.

Toward the end of the nineteenth century, Protestant missioners—German and Swiss Lutherans and American Baptists—came into the Hak-ka territory. They were zealous apostolic men and women, expert educators, doctors and nurses. They established first-rate hospitals, many outstanding schools, and numerous Christian communities.

The Hak-ka Mission

Ford was particularly grateful for the generous way he was treated by the French Fathers. Bishop Rayssac of Swatow had turned over to the Maryknollers five well-equipped parishes, and five others less completed, as well as thirty-seven small chapels and eleven elementary schools. "A pleasant and delicate feature of our taking over this mission," Ford wrote, "is that we have been considered (by the French Fathers) as confreres. That is, everything has been left in its place, undisturbed, which means that we take over very well-furnished houses, including bedclothes and tableware. All we have to do is to light a match to the stove and to the lamp in the dining room and begin to eat." In the central city of the mission, however, that is, in Kaying proper, there were no established chapels, schools, or residences for the missioners.

One of the pioneer Maryknollers among the Hak-kas, Father William Downs of Erie, Pennsylvania, sent back an early appraisal to his superior at Maryknoll: "This is truly

76

an exemplary mission," he wrote, "and all praise for its existence is due to the first two priests of the Paris Foreign Mission Society who sacrificed their lives for Kaying and for the district surrounding it."

Living conditions for the missioners could not be described in terms as glowing, however. Apart from the few rectories left by the French Fathers, the mission homes, Ford's included, were Chinese farmhouses or shops in the main streets of the principal towns. Ford preferred a quiet entrance into an area and thought that renting a shop was better than starting off with an elaborate building program, even if he had had the funds to build. And he personally found excitement in living in a style as close as possible to the local conditions. As he put it, "Half the fun of mission life is lost when men become enslaved by modern conveniences."

Whether one likes to admit it or not, however, the ordinary missioner's mode of life was, and sometimes still is, "colonial" in style. Although it was true that in Kaying Ford and the other Maryknoll missioners had very little money with which to do any building, it was obvious to the local people that the missioner was much beter off than they.

In an April 1927 article Ford gave an indication of his idea of comfort. "Our present quarters," he said, "were sensibly built for one priest, it is a house of five rooms. Into this space we have squeezed a Chinese priest, two Maryknollers, two teachers, and seven minor seminarians. By turning the 'parlor' into a classroom, having the students eat with us and sleep on the porch, we can manage nicely until the new term presents more candidates. Then we may have to find more adequate quarters." But Ford was never convinced that the missioner needed comfortable living quarters to be an effective apostle. Having lived on the barest necessities so long, further sacrifice became easy for him.

On one occasion, visiting a parish in a neighboring town, he was disappointed to discover the priest was away on a mission trip. Ford spent the night there and in the morning after Mass he looked for some coffee and bread. There was neither in the rectory. "I'm not an epicurean, even as missioners go," he conceded, "I could do without a tablecloth, and I rather like to use chopsticks, so I didn't miss the silver, but I haven't yet gotten to the stage where coffee and bread are not a part of breakfast."

He then goes on to describe the missioner's room, a combination bedroom and study.

> The room is not too bad. It has a framed picture of the Pope and an American Cardinal and a holy picture as decoration for the walls, a table, two chairs, a bed and a washbasin . . . There was an open dictionary on the table and several sheets of paper with Chinese characters scratched on them which showed encouraging signs of study.
>
> I smiled as I sat down in the more comfortable chair. Here was a room that the poorest at home would consider unfurnished, and yet I realized there was not a Chinese in the neighborhood but would have considered it very well equipped. While the missioner was trying to become a Chinese in as many ways as possible, in some degree he was living much better than the best of his flock. The missioner had a room all to himself; he had privacy, plenty of food, a servant, and a window in his wall for light and air.

Ford wrote: "The field of this new Maryknoll venture is alluring." And then exuberantly he goes on to say:

"Taking up work among a strange people, meeting new conditions, learning a new language should be a strain. It actually is a relaxation, accompanied by a freshness and delight." He was amazed to find that his few Catholics would walk three and four hours to attend Sunday Mass. He noted that compared to the people of Yeungkong, the Hak-kas were "better off economically"—funds were occasionally coming from the family representatives abroad; they were thus able to build rather large and well-constructed adobe houses. They were "better educated" and had a thirst for learning. This meant it was easier to enlist well-qualified catechists with high school education; it also meant that normally there would be fewer idle young men to form bands of bandits to harass the area, for either they would go abroad or they could obtain gainful employment at home.

It did not take Ford long to love his new people. "My probation here was shorter [than in Yeungkong], because by now I have mastered the simpler forms of politeness." In the March 1927 Maryknoll magazine he said Kaying possessed "an air of buoyant, smiling hope, the atmosphere of the dawn of a long and happy day." Then he went on to say: "Perhaps we can claim for it no more than many other fields; but, for us, Kaying resounds to the music of laughter, to the gaiety of children, to the promise of solid growth and steady progress. We sing a song of youth and gaze upon a scene which means most to us when we envision its tomorrow."

There is no doubt about it, occasionally some wishful thinking creeps into Ford's writings. In 1926 he wrote, somewhat naively, "The Chinese whom we meet know our purpose in coming and our disinterested motives; they know the simplicity of our living compared with commercial agents, and they exaggerate the sacrifices we have been called upon to make. We are receptive and they make the first advances in showing attachment. And we begin to chant in wonder the canticle that our lot is cast in pleasant pastures." Already he had forgotten the Yeungkong anti-foreign demonstrations and was inclined to generalize—because of the genial friends he made—that all Chinese accepted him as a friend.

The hospitable manner in which so many of his Hak-ka hosts treated him recalled to his sensitive mind, and contrasted markedly with, the way his fellow Americans frequently treated Chinese in the United States. Their peaceful resignation to the insulting, unjust discrimination of those days should have won for the Chinese immigrant in America much fairer treatment and high admiration. In a letter to Father James Anthony Walsh, written in May 1926, Ford expressed his deep concern: "Wherever competition with the white man enters, the Chinese has no redress against the laws that are framed to restrict his energies, for he normally does not meddle in politics. In the United States and Canada, he has patiently suffered indignities . . . expulsion without cause . . . neglect, petty annoyances . . . yet in America he has contributed to the progress of our country." Then he adds: "It is a pity that throughout the world the Chinese has not been given a chance to prove his worth. Friendly rivalry would have made his contribution an asset to us . . . is it any wonder that China heretofore has been suspicious of our trade, humiliated by 'foreign concessions' and angered by the 'unequal treaties?' "

Ford in this letter was getting closer to the actual feelings of the Chinese. In a report to Maryknoll in 1928, after speaking of the missioner's busy schedule, the pressing demands, he returns to his favorite theme. He was determined to disabuse his readers of that foolish, smug, self-defeating notion that the Chinese mind hung from the treetops by its tail. "We come to China," he said, "not to barbarians, not to a ruder race. . . . We come to China to a civilization at least comparable to our own—and thousands of years older. . . . We come to a conservative people who understandably do not welcome the missioner, for they do not hope to be bettered by his presence. The missioner should come, not as an equal, but as a humble guest, and a humble student of their language and culture."

One Soul or One Church?

When Ford arrived in Kaying in 1925, the baptismal records showed that there were some four thousand Catholics scattered over his vast territory—about one Catholic for every eight hundred and fifty inhabitants. Not a very significant percentage, to say the least. During Maryknoll's first few years in Kaying there were relatively few converts. This rather disappointed Ford and he felt compelled to explain the slow progress. In the March 1926 Maryknoll magazine, he pointed out that "in this mission we have as many Catholics as in Kongmoon and Wuchow [Maryknoll's other two South China missions at that time] . . . ; this means that for two or three years we shall be busy simply taking care of our present Catholics. Even with Fathers Downs and Malone, we shall be but four men; if we had one more, preferably two, early in 1926 rather than in the fall, it would put us on our feet." Frequently he referred to this "pitiable shortage of priests," explaining that the long hours and days spent away from the central mission to visit the Christian families in distant villages created a situation in which "the missioner lacked the energy to give pagans the attention they deserved."

A few years later someone in America wrote to him with reference to the rather slow rate of conversions. His answer was published in the Maryknoll magazine in September 1932. "The question is this: Why send missioners to places that are hard to convert? Why not concentrate them among the simple savages where thousands instead of hundreds might be baptized each year?" He admitted that this was a fair question. As a young missioner in Yeungkong, Ford had emphasized that the gathering of individual converts was the principal object of his apostolate. Ten years later he had altered his point of view. Evidently, he was being influenced by the papal documents of Benedict XV and Pius XI. He agreed that if the converting of souls were the main object of mission work we should have to submit that "missions in Alaska and Japan are less profitable than missions, for example, in parts of Africa." But then he asks:

> Is the conversion of souls really the main immediate object of the Church? If so, why keep priests at home to minister to Catholics? Why not send every priest to pagan peoples? Evidently there is a reason for the Church's present system, and it appears to be this: the object of mission work is not primarily to convert pagans, it is to establish the Catholic Church in pagan lands. The purpose is to preach the gospel and to build up as complete an organization as possible, which will itself later continue with better success the work of converting the native population.

In conclusion he states: "Even were the whole mission field to prove a failure in respect to converts, it would still be worthwhile as following out our Saviour's command to preach the gospel to all nations." The few hundred gathered for Mass represented for him the entire nation, one part standing for the whole.

Following Ford's arrival in China there had been issued several outstanding papal documents dealing with the missions, beginning with Benedict XV's *Maximum Illud*, and Ford frequently quoted them to his missioners. "It would be regrettable indeed were any missioners to be so forgetful of their dignity as to think more of their earthly than of their heavenly country . . . This would undermine his authority among the people. . . ." On this point Benedict XV's encyclical went on to explain that if the missioner were in any way preoccupied with worldly interests instead of acting in everything like an apostolic man, then he would appear to further the interests of his own country and the native people would at once suspect his intentions. Ford made the encyclicals of the popes the subject for many of his conferences to his missioners. In many of his views Ford seemed to have anticipated Vatican II's Decree on Mission Activity.

How he would have taken to heart Pope John XXIII's words addressed to the 1960 Pax Romana assembly in Manila: "Today it is incumbent upon you, among others, to accept the challenge of translating the message of truth and love into forms appropriate to the oriental mind." Or Pope Paul VI's words spoken on the occasion of the Uganda Martyrs' Canonization in 1964 which read like a page from one of Ford's mission conferences:

> It is our duty, a duty of love, to approach these peoples in a more fraternal dialogue, to give them tokens of our esteem and affection, to show them how the Catholic Church understands their legitimate aspirations, to contribute to their free and honest development in the peaceful paths of human brotherhood,

and thus to make access easier for them, where they fully so desire, to the knowledge of that Christ whom we believe is real salvation for everyone, the original and marvellous interpreter of their own deep aspiration.

Ford believed that "the establishment of the Church" was the missioner's primary objective. This did not mean for him, as it did for so many missioners, the construction of churches, schools, and hospitals. For him it meant the training and development of a native clergy. He would use the laity, but in practice his was to be a priest-centered Church. He realized, of course, that without converts there could be no Christian families from which candidates for the priesthood would come. And so he rejoiced with every increase in the number of his Christians.

During his first furlough to America, Ford gave a talk to the seminarians at St. Mary's Seminary in Baltimore. He admitted that "converts are rather few." Then he added, "But in my ten years in China, I baptized a little over 4,000 people. The majority of these were babies; there were about twelve hundred adults. This shows you that the work isn't fruitless."

But he wasn't satisfied, for he asked: "Must I give up my ideals of being a missioner to pagans?" This was the tantalizing question that he asked himself when he counted the relatively meager increase in his mission statistics, and observed this slow physical-numerical growth. "Is this all there is to the apostolate? A sail on the ocean main usually connotes activity, at least motion, but actually there are long periods of calm when progress is so unnoticeable that we cannot say we are moving, especially if we have no other ship in sight for comparison. So on the missions," he reasons, "we set ourselves to the daily task with long days of simple duties, and the day we baptize a pagan is a red-letter day in the month. . . . St. Francis Xavier was physically exhausted with the pouring of baptismal water, and we are obliged to be content with a solitary convert."

The soul searching went on and he said: "This gives rise to the harrowing thought which refuses to be settled. For years the question colors our view, it is the hardest I have struggled with and it is this: Am I by any chance lacking the power of converting souls?"

In the Maryknoll mission magazine of September 1932, he addressed himself to the question: "Do missioners get results?"—an obvious indication that he had statistics on his mind, even though he did not wish to have the mission of Kaying judged solely from the point of view of its slow numerical increase. After mentioning the fact that two of his seminarians had been ordained priests that year and his parishes had averaged thirty-one adult converts per priest, he answers his own question this way:

> It all depends on what results you are looking for The foreign missions, after all, are the Catholic Church in pagan lands, and the work of the Catholic Church is very hard to measure and weigh and put down in black and white. There are two sides to any work of the Church; the spiritual and the material, and when dealing with a movement extending over centuries it is extremely difficult to just pick out any one period and ask if it is successful even in a material way.

The Master Plan

To help Father Ford with the overwhelming task of Christianizing the territory entrusted to him, in 1928 two

Chinese priests were added to the mission staff, and in the same year Maryknoll sent to Kaying five newly ordained priests and two Brothers.

With respect to the role of Brothers in the apostolate, Ford had written in the Maryknoll mission magazine,

"In our mission work there is a big opportunity for young American Brothers, both in mission centers and in the more remote mission stations. There are schools to be staffed, institutions to be managed, and there is much mission work now performed by priests which the Brothers could share. In school work the Brothers could relieve the priests as head of the school system in a mission. In specialized schools—such as industrial and agricultural schools—a knowledge of the sciences taught would be required. . . . On the mission field the Brother could often take the place of the priest in making visitations, examining catechumens, investigating new openings and superintending the construction of chapels. . . . But there are special qualifications that will make a Brother valuable in mission work. He should be young, not over thirty-five, in good physical condition, of a cheerful frame of mind, able to stand alone, and have some taste for study. Such qualities are not hard to find in our American young men."

But Maryknoll had very few Brothers in those days, so Ford was unable to put his program for the Brothers into operation. The two Brothers assigned to Maryknoll became ill shortly after arriving and they were never replaced.

With the enlargement of his staff Ford was ready to make a serious bid for the minds and souls of the Hak-ka people. During his seven years in Yeungkong, he had been experimenting, trying various methods, appraising the Chinese people, studying their history and their culture. The task before him, he knew, was a monumental one. He studied the territory and the people, measured the problems, made his plans, and prepared to face the challenge. There in Kaying he had, as he said, "in one kaleidoscope the history of twenty centuries; the primitive Church, the age of persecutions, the unfolding of dogmas, the questions of national rites, the incorporation of Catholic terms in a new language, the baptizing of pagan customs, and the development of a native Church."

The basic obstacle was the Chinese himself. As Ford put it in a letter to Maryknoll: "The ordinary Chinese doesn't care whether or not we come to evangelize him; the average pagan thinks we're here because China is more attractive to us than our own homeland. Or worse still, many pagans feel we have come because of the fat salary our government gives us to exploit them in some way." In a word, they thought missioners were in China for their own advantage and that no good could come to China from it. To Ford, altering that attitude was a challenge to be approached with confidence, not a problem to be faced with alarm.

The progress of the mission, he felt, would be in direct proportion to his success in mobilizing the total membership, with every Christian working toward the spread of the faith. The timeless message and the divine command were clear enough: "Teach all nations." The method of conveying the message and following the command changes with each nation and each sector of its society, and to a certain extent, with each individual.

Ford laid out four broad areas that formed his overall master plan of action: (1) He would train as many qualified and willing lay helpers as possible to participate personally and directly in the apostolate. (2) He would immediately establish a seminary to train young Chinese men for the priesthood, and a novitiate to prepare Chinese women for the religious life. (3) He would invite Maryknoll Sisters to take up work in the area, not merely to direct orphanages or other institutions of charity, but to go out to the women of China and preach the gospel to them. (4) He would have his missioners engage in direct evangelization using the written word as well as personal contact with non-Christians.

The Laity

There is among the Chinese in general a tendency toward group action. The trait can have advantages in the apostolate as it unites the scattered Christian families and gives them an influence far beyond their numerical strength. Where there was no priest available for Sunday Mass, Ford prepared a program of prayers and hymns to be conducted by the village Catholic leader, or by a catechist trained in his Catechetical School in Kaying. In his Catechist School, he followed the method of St. Augustine. As he explained in an article for the Homeletic and Pastoral Review in 1940, "St. Augustine emphasized the need of presenting Catholic doctrine, not as a dry skeleton of well-articulated truths, but as an expression of God's love for us and ours for Him, prefigured in Old Testament history and living in the Age of Christ, continuing on in the history of the Church. He combines liturgy, Bible history and the catechism to give us a well-rounded insight into man's place in God's scheme."

The Christians were reminded of their responsibilities to live the gospel and to pass it on to others. Each Christian was to be a witness. In Ford's mind this was never to be reduced simply to the proclamation of the gospel. The catechist was to live out what he believed in the presence of the non-Christian: he was to walk with the new Christian on the hard and wonderful road from unbelief to joyful certainty. Just as Ford exhorted his missioners, so too did he tell his convert leaders, "You are not only messengers, but also Christbearers."

The village leaders read the Scriptures and followed the prepared course of instruction, announcing what God had done in Christ, rather than what they thought the message should be or what they thought of the message. Catechists, leaders, ordinary Christians, Ford would use them all—all should participate in the salvific mission of the Church in their own environment. Every baptized and confirmed member of the Church was called to witness to the truth of God. In the Kaying mission the laity had a further task beyond bearing witness and instructing. Ford held frequent meetings with them and sought their advice; and, at times, he followed their advice even when it was contrary to the opinion of his priests.

The Seminary

One of the reasons why, after three centuries of effort, the number of Chinese Catholics was still small was the lack of any coordinated attempts to train a Chinese secular clergy. As early as 1630, the Congregation of Propaganda urged the missioners to discover "the most intelligent among the Christians" and to "raise them to Holy Orders, up to and including the priesthood." Yet the few Chinese men who became priests belonged to religious orders whose superiors were located outside the country. According to available correspondence, most European missioners apparently believed that the Chinese character was too weak to embrace the responsibility of the priesthood and so they did not encourage vocations. Francis Ford knew better, and so did his contemporaries, the famous Lazarist missioners, Fathers Vincent Lebbé and Anthony Cotta. Father Lebbé, in fact, had a marked influence on the mission thinking of Popes Benedict XV and Pius XI, whose directives in turn influenced Ford and supported what he already believed: without Chinese priests the Church would be like a rice plant which sprouts but does not flower. "If the Church in China is to take root and flourish," he said, "it is necessary to concern ourselves with finding vocations for the priesthood from among the flock entrusted to our care." Only the native clergy would guarantee the growth and permanency of the Church. Thus, the development of a seminary was of primary importance in Ford's overall plan for his Kaying mission.

When Ford arrived in Kaying in 1925, he found eight boys waiting to begin their training for the priesthood. He resolved to accept them and he started the "seminary" in his rented, somewhat cramped quarters. He says, "Of course, our conscience whispered that we should not start in so inadequate a place, but we were deaf." He took the boys in and, like the schools of Charlemagne, the students became part of the household.

The following year, more boys came, and so, as he put it: "The battle was taken out of our hands. We now have twenty-one seminarians, and it is impossible to house them in a two-bedroom dwelling." Strictly speaking it was not impossible, for he was doing it, but at the sacrifice of order and discipline. No one but a Chinese boy would have put up with the discomforts incidental to those narrow quarters. Ford conceded that it was rather a bold step to start to build a seminary without funds and to attempt to staff it without personnel, and, he added, "I suspect a still bolder step is to ask for the money."

At any rate, as he related in a 1927 letter to Maryknoll, he had "decided to build the seminary for the Maryknoll Hak-ka mission even now in our second year of entrance into this field." He was confident this would be, in the long run, the answer to his personnel plight and the answer to the permanent establishment of the Church in China. "Future generations," he confidently predicted, "may point with pride to the foresight of the pioneers, and mention the seminary as an instance of their zeal for native vocations." Even so, because of his lack of money, he wished it to be a matter of record for truth's sake that "we are building against our will."

The young missioner had always been scrupulously careful of the limited amount of money Maryknoll could send him. He assured his superiors at Maryknoll that he was not wasting money on foolish schemes.

He admitted that when he had reached Kaying one of his first resolutions had been "not to build anything anywhere until we were well settled both in knowledge of the area and in fluency in the language, and also until we had adequate funds." This promise to do nothing until his financial credit warranted it, was, he said, an axiom he borrowed from Ben Franklin, for experience had shown that "early wrinkles and gray hairs are the result of living up to one's income without any reserve."

Ford's good resolution had to be broken. "The Guardian Angel of the mission," he wrote, "surely must have smiled at our simplicity. . . . We poor mortals were trying to imitate the 'children of this world' in being prudent, but that no flesh might glory in itself, Providence simply stepped in and ran things from God's viewpoint and we were helpless." Priestly vocations came much faster than the mission had dared hope, and when he received a copy of Pope Pius XI's encyclical pleading with mission bishops not to refuse vocations that seemed to be genuine, he no longer accused himself of imprudence.

And so, not knowing where he would get the money to build it, or the professors to staff it, Ford launched forth into the construction of the Kaying seminary, on the outskirts of the city, about three miles from the temporary cathedral parish church. He made an honest attempt, following the injunction of the Apostolic Delegate and his own strong convictions on the subject, to adapt Chinese architectural style to the building. Up to this time most of the Catholic missioners in China had been Europeans, and when they constructed a church they copied the lines of the best European cathedrals. Ford wished to erect a building that would take Chinese artistic taste and ennoble it by consecrating it to God. He would use the characteristic Chinese roof with two concave converging lips culminating in a massive horizontal ridge with projecting, upturned eaves. The school would provide five classrooms, a dining room, a library, a dormitory large enough for fifty students and six bedrooms for the teaching staff.

Writing to Maryknoll with understandable satisfaction, he said: "The building is still in the rough, and much remains to be done to complete the details; but at least, even now, it is not out of harmony with its surroundings. It seems to fit into the bamboo background; and viewed from a distance, with the Hak-ka hills behind it, its mottled colors melt into the scene. It is greenish brown and will darken more with time and the weather."

When Father William Downs first saw the seminary, he was amazed at the "splendid piece of work." He wrote to

Maryknoll acclaiming Ford's talents as an architect. The building reminded him of the major seminary at Maryknoll, New York.

Years later, in 1944, Bishop James E. Walsh visited the Kaying seminary when he was Superior General of Maryknoll. "The Kaying mission," he wrote, "has one building. The building is the seminary with the missioners living in odd corners."

Ford continually emphasized the responsibility of each missioner to cultivate as many vocations as possible. On his visits to the seminary, watching the young men at study or at play or at prayer, he dreamt of "the fair prospects of a native clergy who would evangelize the region." He envisaged the day when the Hak-ka valleys would be dotted with chapels, staffed by Chinese priests. The training of these future priests was so important in his eyes, that, as he said, "We must go forward, even blindly if necessary, in this work."

To have Chinese priests all over his Hak-ka mission— this was the dream that obsessed him, this was the goad that drove him on. He never wanted the Church in Kaying to walk a treadmill and he foresaw the day, not too distant, when Maryknoll priests would not be thinking of doing things *for* the Kaying Church, but *with* it and *through* it. He had no intentions of bypassing the native Church. He would nurture it and put it on its own two feet as quickly as it could stand alone. For him the overall object was not merely to get things done, not merely to establish institutions that would be financed and staffed from America; he wanted the native Christianity to live in a climate that would permit it to grow in responsibility. Oversimplifying, perhaps, the missioner's objective, he planned a Church so well knit that its sole aim could be expressed in a single idea: "The raising up of a native clergy." "Given a native clergy," he added, "China is as Catholic as Rome itself and it is then only a question of time. Time is accidental; a clergy is the essential element."

Ford's first few years in his Hak-ka mission were devoted to the seminary. There was no question but what he was proud of this venture: "We feel our Kaying Mission is well begun and solidly founded in our little seminary, and without exception our men have put their best efforts toward its success. Materially, as yet, it is a poor infant; financially, it has been a heavy expense for a still unknown mission to bear; and the running of it has demanded care; yet it is the pain akin to parenthood that gives an outlet for the love we need to express, and we would not wish it otherwise."

No one appreciated more than Bishop Ford the triumph of raising a Chinese boy to God's altar, and because, in his eyes, the making of a priest was the sublimist of works, the training of Chinese young men for the priesthood and their work as priests were personally directed and closely watched by him. "A Chinese priest," he wrote in the Maryknoll magazine, "naturally should take his normal place among his own people, fit into the mosaic of their lives without stress or strain; his position as leader of his flock depends to a great extent, of course, on his personal character. Given the proper training, he should be able to lead his people as no foreigner can. Should he lack important natural qualities, however, he may miss many opportunities that a more widely experienced foreign priest will grasp. However, up to the present, by training and character the ordinary Chinese priest seems less venturesome than the foreigner when he is off the beaten path and outside the daily routine."

Conscious of his responsibility to prepare his Hak-ka priest candidates to take their place as leaders in the community, he wanted them to avoid the shortcomings he had observed in other Chinese priests. It was his conviction that "the Chinese priest could know much more about the pagan religions in his country, more about Chinese history, art and music, to say nothing about these matters as they are in other cultures." Since the great majority of the candidates came from rural areas, it was understandable that they might lack the polish and urbanity of youngsters from the city. Ford conceded this. "At the present time the ordinary Chinese priest," he said, "understands the importance of the weather changes on crops much more keenly than he does the effect of western inventions on the economic life of his country."

"The Chinese priest," observed Ford, "has not been up to now a good mixer in the American sense of the term; he has lived for the most part within the walls of the Church property; he is seldom seen in the marketplace or at civil functions." Analyzing the causes for this attitude and determining to amend the condition in his Kaying seminary, Ford did not lay the blame at the feet of the Chinese clergy. "To judge the situation rightly," he said, "We must take into account two factors; the training given the clerical students and the Chinese character." Most priests, he said, were village boys who had been brought up in the shelter of Catholic homes, protected from pagan influences. This in itself could have been overcome, but the weakness of the curriculum in most seminaries was lack of preparation in the Chinese classics, history, and culture, and neglect of the modern sciences. Ford would correct these deficiencies in his Kaying seminary. The Chinese priests who were subsequently trained in the Kaying seminary during the rectorship of Fathers Eckstein, Donnelly, Hilbert, and Tsong, are a testimony to Ford's vision.

The young men in the Kaying seminary were trained

not only in their pastoral duties. They were to be ordained not only to serve the flock handed over to them by the foreign missioners, they were themselves to be missioners, alert to openings, alive to opportunities, exploring possibilities, reaching out to new villages for new converts. They were to be vessels of election carrying Christ's Name to their non-Christian fellow countrymen. Ford reminded his Maryknollers that it was their responsibility to set the pattern, to give the apostolic example to the young Chinese priests. He pointed out that the Chinese priests' "idea of priestly work will be derived from our manner of thinking and talking and acting."

It is a tribute to Ford's fatherly direction that the relationship between the Maryknollers and the Chinese priests was without discord or dissension. If a minor misunderstanding did arise, the bishop would invariably side with the Chinese. He would become indignant at the sight of jealousies, enmities, or divisions among his priests. These represented a spirit antagonistic to the spirit of an apostle and were a great offense to him. There was opposition enough from the outside; there was to be no opposition from within.

When the seminarians completed their course in the Kaying seminary, they attended the Regional Seminary in Hong Kong, under the direction of the Irish Jesuit Fathers, for their final six years of study before ordination. (This splendid institution overlooking Aberdeen harbor has now been closed for lack of Chinese students.) A former rector of the Hong Kong seminary once referred to the Kaying Diocese as "the best friend the seminary had among all the places from which the seminarians came. They were better prepared and always ready to cooperate. Bishop Ford had a greater understanding of our difficulties and a greater appreciation of our work than any of the other bishops of our region."

This is how Ford expressed the problem of a national clergy in a 1933 Maryknoll magazine article: "A country without a native clergy, or having an insufficient native priesthood, is always in danger of being stranded for lack of a pilot. In time of persecution the first to be wiped out or driven out is the foreigner. A tree that cannot keep its roots intact during a typhoon is doomed. The problem then of a native clergy in mission lands is not one merely of logical expediency, but of the utmost urgency. The bishops (in China) have begun to realize this during the past decade. . . . They have multiplied the number of native seminaries and have more than doubled the number of students." While the education of Chinese seminarians was a long and costly one—since they covered the same courses as seminarians in America—the standards had unfortunately not always been maintained. However, after ten years in China Ford could observe a marked improvement and concluded that he was "witnessing the real beginning of the solution of the problem."

Ford did not intend his Chinese priests to be second rate—he wanted them to be as adequately prepared as possible. A well-prepared priest would never suffer from timidity or narrow-mindedness, the qualities which Ford felt "never draws souls to God." At one time he considered sending some of his candidates to Peking, but demurred because the information he had was "too vague as to their courses and discipline." Several students he sent to Rome for theology and graduate work.

Father Marcus Chai, who was ordained in Rome in 1933, expressed his grateful joy in a letter back to Kaying: "On Christmas day I said Mass at St. Peter's and applied it for all the Maryknollers in the Kaying Mission and for Monsignor Ford, my teacher and father, my benefactor and superior." When Chai returned from Rome, Ford appointed him director of a students' hostel and editor of the mission's influential monthly *Sin Nam Sen*. (Today Father Chai, now a Doctor of Philosophy, is the president of a college on Taiwan.)

Another student from the Kaying seminary to be ordained in Rome in 1941 was Father Paul Lam, who had this to say about his journey to the priesthood: "I was the first student admitted to the Kaying seminary, where I studied for nine years. . . . Afterwards I was sent to Hong Kong to begin the study of philosophy and finally I was enrolled here in Rome in the college of *Propaganda Fidei*. . . . My first Mass was one of thanksgiving for all the Maryknollers who have made it possible for me to go up to the altar of God." At the end of World War II Father Lam returned from Rome. He taught in the Kaying seminary, became Vicar General of the diocese, and later succeeded Bishop Ford as the superior of the Kaying Mission when Ford was arrested and imprisoned.

Step Three: Sisters

Father Ford had read many objections to and adverse criticisms of missionary work in China; that it was not efficient; that there was very little to show for three centuries of evangelization; that a generation is converted only to die out leaving little impression on the next generation; that no one had succeeded in establishing a permanent Chinese Church. "These are serious objections," he admitted. "But to face the problem squarely, we must admit a serious defect in our system of evangelization and it is this: until recent times we had very few Sisters in

China and our work among both pagans and Christians was lopsided; our neglect of the women aggravated the traditional apathy of the Chinese themselves for the welfare of their women." He had noticed that when the wives of Christian husbands did not come in contact with the Church, superstitions were ritually carried out in the home, and the daughters in these families were often betrothed to non-Christians. Missioners had concentrated on the conversion of the men and did not insist—as he did—that the wives and mothers enter the Church with the men.

And it was precisely here he said, "the weakness of our attack lies. The worship of idols is left nowadays almost exclusively to the zeal of women, or, at least, they are the backbone of idolatry; the men are more indifferent, content with superstitions on a minor scale or on special occasions. . . . Had we won over the women to the true worship during the past three centuries, the Church would have had a far more glorious tale to tell." That there were few really Christian families, missioners could not, of course, entirely be blamed, for it was almost impossible to reach the women. Accepted custom and rigid etiquette forbade men to talk with women who were not members of the family.

Up to the end of World War II Chinese women traditionally had been segregated from the opposite sex and, in public, isolated from social contact with men. In the twenties there was considerable literature published in China on the rights of women and the need for emancipation and there was some progress made in the port cities. However, little was done before World War II to change the status of women in the rural area. Except in the large coastal Westernized cities, it was unusual to see even a husband and wife walking side by side on the street; and still more unusual to see a woman talking with a man who was not a relative. Ford appreciated the difficulty this fact created for the mission. To have a priest visit the homes of non-Christians in an attempt to interest the women of the family in the doctrine would be contrary to the local traditions. He felt that the sheltered, secluded nature of the woman's life in China called for consecrated women who would be able to penetrate the woman's world of the household. This was a task, he felt, that Sisters could well undertake. They would have access to the women and girls, they would be able to enlist the entire family, instruct them, console them, lead them. Having watched with joy the work of the Maryknoll Sisters in his former mission in Yeungkong, he knew that the solution to the problem would be the enrollment of Sisters for this branch of the apostolate. And so he petitioned the Mother General of the Maryknoll Sisters to send a group to Kaying. The request was readily granted.

The original group of six, under the leadership of Sister Mary Imelda Sheridan, left for Kaying in 1933. Ford met the group in Swatow and personally escorted them up river. His first commission to them was to learn well the Chinese language. And learn it they did by diligent application to hard study for long hours day and night. Ford also instructed them to learn all they could about the customs of the Chinese women and their families—their habits, likes and dislikes, their pet peeves and their aspirations. They were to be ready to live with them, to rejoice with them, to comfort them, guide them. They were to win their confidence and their affection. Hours must be spent reviewing theology and scripture. The latest catechetical system must be acquired to enable them to explain Christianity fittingly and in a manner acceptable to Chinese women.

Ford was insistent on the necessity of studying the

culture of China. He knew that some of his missioners felt that they could not understand the Chinese people, that the Chinese were inscrutable. He considered this a sign of the missioner's failure to study China's traditions and culture; for when a missioner found a people inscrutable, it was invariably because he was uninformed about them. Ford, as a young missioner, had had to grapple with social institutions he did not at first understand and to wrestle with deep prejudices, habits of thought and action undreamed of before he arrived in Yeungkong.

The struggle was partially resolved by reading all he could find on China's past. He tried to understand the history, the traditions, the mores, the mentality of the Chinese people. Diligently he practiced looking at things from their point of view. And he wanted his staff to do likewise. How else would their words make sense to their listeners in serious discussion? How else could they create an atmosphere for a real human dialogue? To the Sisters Ford emphasized the importance of knowing the interests, convictions, doubts, and worries of the Chinese women in order to develop sympathy and understanding. This study was to be for the Sisters a lifelong process. The particular situations of each of the Chinese women were to be understood and taken seriously, so that the gospel message could be related and in turn be taken seriously. They must create an atmosphere of truly human intercourse before they could offer the message of Christ.

The Sisters were to be ready to go out into distant villages for days on end visiting Christians and instructing them. They would then invite to the mission the prospective women converts in the "off season"—the weeks between the planting and harvesting—to instruct them in the teachings and the liturgy of the Church. Convent rules might have to be adjusted, religious schedules might have to be adapted to the needs of the people, but the Sisters were to be at the service of the women and children at all times. "Get out among the people," Ford directed them, "go into their homes. Tell the women and children about God and Christ."

Heretofore, with heroic and edifying dedication, most missionary Sisters in China, like those in Yeungkong, had confined their activities to needed works of charity—orphanages, old folks homes, and hospitals. But Ford was determined to train the Maryknoll Sisters for the direct apostolate and to keep them free to preach the gospel. They would visit the sick and give medical aid as best they could in a modest, nonprofessional way; but he did not want the Sisters in his mission at that time to become tied down to an institution.

Ford reserved the training of the Sisters for himself, for, along with the seminary, this was a project especially close to his heart. He found time to direct a detailed five-year language course for them and to guide the preparation of their activities. His frequent conferences to the Sisters evidenced his deep spirituality and his practical view of life. He outlined for them the moral tone of the pagan society in which they were to live and work. He wished them to face reality without being shocked, to keep in mind the need to have a personal reverence for all God's creatures for whom Christ died. He quoted a remark once made to him by Bishop Fulton Sheen: "It is only in attention to the individual's need that you clinch his attention." Then Ford added his own observation that an impersonal attitude never attracts: "I've noticed those who make few converts are often men who seem indifferent to others, though faithful otherwise in their duties."

Another error to be forestalled was the Western

tendency to restless, rash zeal. The Sisters were to learn that the Chinese prefer to move along unruffled and unhurried in low gear, which, as Ford said, "is the best in climbing hills and on the slippery paths of life. And," he added, "the Chinese have no need for yearly stylish modifications." Chinese peasants travelled on foot over dirt paths; they knew nothing of four lane highways. The women among whom the Sisters were to begin their work knew little of the outside world. The complexities of politics, the advances in science did not disturb them. The sun rose and the sun set, but they had no desire to train a telescope upon a star. Their children got sick and mysteriously died, but they never thought to turn a microscope upon a drop of stagnant water. The young students, it is true, were quite different. Their restless intellects wanted to catch up with the speeding world and to penetrate the secrets of the universe. But for the time being, the Sisters would concentrate on the uneducated women in their village homes.

Ford reminded the Sisters of the high price Christ paid for each soul. Consolations were to be mixed with disappointments. "The joy of a missionary Sister," he told them, "must be mixed with gall and wormwood, and must bear heavy on her strength." He was confident that their efforts would be crowned with success. This was to be the price of victory: the smarting marks of the combat would become the joy of the rainbow seen through the storm.

As a father prepares his children for the realities of a cruel and ruthless world, Ford continually spoke to the Sisters of the dangers and difficulties they might encounter. "No matter how dark the world around us, no matter how overwhelming the task ahead of us," he counselled, "the thought that 'God is good' can send us smiling through life. We have the uproarious secret with which to thwart the devil and all his vanities. We know the answers to life's riddles and we can afford to smile at so-called calamities. Like children playing hide-and-seek with God, we know we shall be caught by God and taken into His embrace, and life becomes literally a game and a test and even a hard endurance test, but with the consciousness that God is judge and watching from the side-lines, that God Himself is the prize."

The Sisters entered into the physically taxing program with joyous enthusiasm. In hot, humid South China the Sisters, with their long, flowing, white garb, travelled over the rough mountain roads, rode buses or bicycles, sailed in cramped quarters without privacy in river boats and sampans. They visited the sick, the dying, the poor, the rich, always giving, always reaching out, always smiling, always hopeful that they might plant the seed of faith in the hearts of their listeners.

One day a Maryknoll Sister, her Chinese woman companion, and a priest journeyed to a remote village high in the hills bordering Fukien province. Shortly after they started this walk, about ten in the morning, a heavy tropical rain began to fall. The mountain path became sloppy and slippery. The driving rain continued, soaking Sister's habit. Her small umbrella protected only her veil and headpiece. Her shoes oozed mud and water. Yet through the day's long ordeal she was as cheerful and buoyant as a young woman on the beach. The small group reached the village as the day was ending. It was the first time the people had ever been visited by a Sister and the non-Christians had never seen her like before. She had not carried a spare habit, and since she obviously could not sit around in her wet clothes, the village women found a Chinese gown, with high collar and slit skirt, that fitted the Sister. Her veil and headpiece looked incongruous over the silk gown and the bedroom slippers, but until late at night Sister spoke to the women about the Lord and how much He loved them.

The Maryknoll Sisters, as they became more fluent in the language and more knowledgeable in the customs, were asked by Bishop Ford to establish a hostel in Kaying for girls attending government middle schools. This was one of the many means used by the Sisters to interest the Chinese women in the Church. The Sisters found that they could reach teachers as well as parents through the students residing at the hostel, and many converts were made to the Church through these contacts.

Francis Ford never tired of lauding the Sisters' zeal. There were few apostolic ventures in Kaying that did not have the Sisters as an integral part of the team. Because Chinese women did most of the worshipping of idols and because they had the most influence on the children in the homes, Ford never ceased to insist: "Missionary Sisters must get to them, and until they do, there will be little real progress for the Church in China."

He spoke about the work of a Sister in a village of fallen away Catholics: "Nothing short of a miracle," he exclaimed. "Priests and catechists had failed. But after she had spent a month in the village forty-nine new converts signed up for the doctrine course and many lax Catholics returned to the Sacraments."

Summing up his evaluation of the Sisters, he reported to Maryknoll: "They have grasped the importance of the direct spiritual action on the people so well, and have mapped it so minutely in detail, that I am beginning to wonder what the Church ever did before they arrived on the missions. When I yield to daydreams and convince myself that Kaying is running at top speed, I have only to remember the impetus the Sisters have given us, and I am completely deflated. I never knew what 'absorbed in work' meant until I saw them in action. That is the beauty of beginning with no traditions to slow them down; they have nothing with which to measure their zeal except their ambitions, and they naturally think they have fallen short."

Just as he was convinced that there was no permanent future in his mission if he did not prepare a native clergy to assume the priestly direction of the people, so was Ford convinced that Chinese Sisters must be trained for the apostolate to share the burden of the work among the women and children. From the moment he built his seminary for priests, he had planned the formation of a native Sisterhood. Troubled local conditions at the time made the undertaking extremely difficult. However, he did not let this obstacle prevent him from sending his prospective candidates to Hong Kong to be trained there by the Maryknoll Sisters. He rented a small house for the fourteen aspirants, recruited from various villages of the Kaying mission, and Sister Mary Dolores began their formation. When conditions quieted down in Kaying, they returned to the mission and began an on-the-job training program working directly with the Maryknoll Sisters.

When drawing up the Constitutions and rules for the new community of Chinese Sisters, a Maryknoll Sister suggested to Ford that he make their purpose "just like ours. Limit them to the direct missionary work among the women and children." And with this as its aim, the Chinese congregation of Sister Catechists was founded. During the period of their novitiate, the novices did not remain cloistered. They spent some time each day in actual mission work. In this way, practical field experience went hand and hand with their intensive spiritual formation.

Ford introduced into the training program of the Chinese Sisters another innovation, which many considered a foolish risk at the time. He decided to enroll the postulants and novices in a top-grade government middle school for girls: "In this way I have no teachers' salaries to pay." When they qualified for a government school, the aspirants were actually given an allowance by the civil authorities. And so, as Ford put it, "We have the unique distinction of government support for our postulants and novices." It was his intention to have the girls, most of them from small villages, mature with other young women of their age. They received at the same time experience of the world into which they would enter as nuns. The government diplomas were an added enrichment. Of course, he saw also some disadvantages in the plan for a secular education. But he felt it was a good test of their vocations. "Besides," he said, "we don't have money for anything else."

The value of this training was to be shown in the exceptional work the Chinese Sisters did in the various parishes throughout the Kaying mission and in their loyalty later, after they were forced from their convents by the Communists and made to return to their native villages dressed in simple peasant garb.

With the establishment of his seminary and the founding of the native Sisters' community, Ford looked forward to years of peace during which he might implement his other plans for the expansion of the mission work. In a letter at that time, he observed that in the Hak-ka region there were fewer bandits than in his Yeungkong mission and that the troublesome skirmishes between warlords were rarer. But he was living in a country and in a time that knew few days of peace.

 # CHAPTER V

LOU TSENG-TSIANG

I have striven all my life, to the best of my ability,
so to behave as to see clearly and to walk straight,
not to let myself knowingly be blinded by any prejudices
or any fear, and perpetually to reconsider my deeds
and my duties in the light of experience, of reflection
and of our common dependence upon Heaven.

Ways of Confucius and of Christ p. 1

SAINT PAUL

Brethren, I have conducted myself before God with
a perfectly good conscience up to this day.

ACTS 23:1

The Rise of Communism

Because Francis Ford was to meet his death at the hands of the Communists, and because the activities of all missioners were to cease under the attempt by the Communists to exterminate all foreign influence, it is germaine to our story to speak briefly of the rise of Communism in China.

In the spring of 1920, a group of intellectuals in Shanghai organized the Marxist Study Association, and here the Chinese Communist Party was conceived. The

Soviet Union's recent revolutionary success, its strong anti-capitalist stand, the magnanimous gesture in relinquishing its special rights in China promised these men that the cure-all for China's foreign and domestic ills was friendship with Russia. In the summer of that year, the Communist Youth Corps was organized and many Chinese students accepted the invitation to go to Moscow for university studies. This was followed in 1921 by the formation of the Communist Party and the First Party Congress held under the direction of Russia's agent, G. Maring. Sun Yat-sen, "the Father of the Republic," was persuaded that his aims and the Communists' aims were the same. Having failed to get financial and technical help from America and Britain, Sun agreed to a formal alliance with the Soviet Union. At the Kuomintang's First Party Congress held in 1924 and organized with the help of political experts from Russia, the Communist delegates pledged their loyalty to Sun Yat-sen as their leader. One Communist, a relatively obscure young man named Mao Tse-tung, was elected an alternate member of the Central Executive Committee of the Kuomintang.

As the Communists gained in numbers, their strong anti-imperialist, and anti-landlord demonstrations increased. Discontents so long dormant, now became active hatreds.

Shortly after Ford arrived in Kaying, Chiang Kai-shek had marched from Canton in the south to exterminate all warlords in an attempt to unify the country. Everyone hoped for peace. But peace is a rare commodity in perennially wartorn China. On May 30th, 1925, during a strike against a Japanese textile mill in Shanghai, the Japanese management shot and killed a Chinese worker and wounded several others. A few days later, during a student anti-foreign demonstration in Shanghai, British soldiers opened fire and killed a number of students. Anti-West feeling exploded in most of the coastal cities. Many hundreds of Chinese were killed. The entire country rose up and united behind Chiang Kai-shek in a spirit of enthusiastic nationalism. However, there followed a split in the Kuomintang, the Nationalist Party. One faction, controlled by the leftists and Communists was violently anti-foreign; by organizing the peasants and workers, they were converting Chiang's Northern Expedition from an anti-warlord campaign into an anti-foreign and a social and economic revolution. Chiang, who represented a more conservative faction of the Kuomintang, felt that the foreign-backed Communists were acutally more of a danger to the country than the warlords. Accordingly he decided, in March of 1927, to change the course of the revolution and to liquidate the Russian-backed Communists, who had been organizing the strikes and demonstrations to prepare in advance for taking over Shanghai.

In 1927 Communist-inspired mobs invaded British and American consulates, killed many foreigners, destroyed Christian churches, and other property owned by foreigners. British and American warships opened fire on Nanking. China appeared to be destined for another slaughter of its people in a Boxer-type reprisal. It was against this background that Chiang Kai-shek struck out against the Communists. Chiang had little difficulty defeating the ill-equipped Communist forces. Chou En-lai, who was in Shanghai at that time organizing the Communist activities there, barely escaped. From this time on Chiang and his Nationalist Kuomintang Party were to be at war with the Communists.

About this time, Chiang became a Christian; he was baptised into the Methodist Church of which his wife was a member. But Chiang's conversion had little effect on the masses. Even his public messages pleading with the people to renounce their backward superstitious practices had little appreciable influence. Although he enjoyed considerable popular support during those days, he had too many problems to face—poverty, illiteracy, disease, and the humiliating presence of foreign troops in China's port cities—and he had too few dedicated men to help him.

The Communists had no intention of giving up. Toward the end of 1927, led by Moscow-trained Li Li-san, they recruited sufficient numbers to stage a series of uprisings against the Nationalist forces in the central and southern areas of China. While these attacks were not militarily successful, they did bring about the union of the Communists' military leader Chu Teh and the political genius Mao Tse-tung; and this coalition became the nucleus upon which the powerful Communist force was eventually built.

While both Sun Yat-sen and Chiang Kai-shek had pledged to right the injustices of the treaties with the Western powers and to rid China of foreign troops, neither had manifested any strong hatred for the West or for the Christian Church. The Communists, on the other hand, made it clear that they believed the Christian missioners were agents of the Western governments striving to subjugate and control their country.

From 1926 to 1928, the Maryknollers in the Hak-ka hills enjoyed relative peace and quiet. However, in October 1928, Communist guerillas sudenly marched down from Fukien and Kiangsi to extend their gains into Kwangtung. The route selected was through the Hak-ka mission.

The parish of Shakchin was the closest to the Fukien border. Its pastor, Father Patrick Malone, wrote to Maryknoll, "My cook came rushing in shouting: 'Father, Father, Red soldiers are coming.' . . . I ran to the Church and while I was consuming the Blessed Sacrament, the Reds were banging on the mission gate." Father Malone took refuge in a neighboring village. He returned the next day when he learned that the Communists had moved on.

Malone's report continued: "The church and house were completely ransacked. The Communists had destroyed what they did not take away. They vented their rage in particular on the church vestments, the sacred vessels, the crucifixes and the tabernacle; . . . about three hundred Reds spent the night in the church . . .; they departed leaving the place in shambles with Red slogans written all over the walls. A German Lutheran missioner, his hands tied behind his back, was led away with them." During these days, Malone's mission, which was on the direct road between Fukien and Kaying, was badly damaged not once, but three times.

The next objective for the Communists was Kaying City. Ford had gone to Hong Kong to attend Maryknoll's first general chapter, after which he made his first visit to America since his 1918 departure. Father William Downs had been left in charge of the mission. Downs sent the seminarians home as a safety measure and he removed most of the sacred vessels and vestments to the homes of Christians in the neighboring villages. When the priests saw the approaching Red army heading for the seminary, they prudently sought safety in a nearby village. "The Communists," Downs wrote, "released all the prisoners in the Kaying jail, burned the court house, printed a Communist newspaper, demanded money from the shopkeepers, and held a mass meeting during which they announced they would burn all buildings in Kaying owned by foreigners at five o'clock that afternoon."

About four o'clock, government troops arrived from Canton and thwarted that plan by driving off the Communists after heavy fighting.

When Ford returned from America a few months later, he was greeted in Kaying with a warm and enthusiastic welcome by the Christians. However, he soon began to notice a certain uneasiness in the atmosphere. Among the students there was considerable anti-foreign sentiment and occasionally they would give expression to it. Ford understood better than he wanted to admit that his beloved Chinese had not completely accepted him as one of their own, nor had they clearly understood the purpose of his presence among them. Undaunted, he reassured Maryknoll about the conditions in his area following the Communist trouble: "Thanks be to God," he wrote, "the harrowing interruption in our work did not continue long. Gradually, as the Nationalist soldiers regained our territory, we reassembled the seminarians and took up again our usual life. The test brought out the solid faith and sympathy of our people, and reassured us of at least the goodwill of some of our non-Christian neighbors."

Monsignor Ford

As a foreign mission society, Maryknoll is directly responsible to the Prefect of the Congregation for the Propagation of the Faith in Rome. The Cardinal Prefect assigns territories under its jurisdiction to various mission societies. Until an area is sufficiently developed, its missioners work under the direction of the bishop governing the mission from which the new territory has been cut off. When the progress warrants it, a superior is appointed by Rome and the area is raised to the status of a "prefecture." In May 1929, word came from Rome that the Hak-ka mission, with Kaying as its See City, had been erected into a prefecture and Father Francis Xavier Ford was nominated its first Prefect Apostolic with the title, Right Reverend Monsignor.

Ford had been the superior of the mission up to that time, but he found it difficult, nonetheless, to accustom himself to his new title "Monsignor" or, as the Chinese called him, "Lord of Religion."

At this time the mission was enjoying a period of relative peace. Ford saw an opportunity to launch out and put into operation his program for making the entire Hakka people Christian.

The 1930's were happy years. Apart from some trouble with his teeth and an occasional upset stomach, the Monsignor's health remained fairly good as he enjoyed a period of tranquility. The present seemed to be moving smoothly and the future held no fears. New missioners were coming annually from Maryknoll. Soon he would have more young Chinese priests. The missioners' annual statistical reports showed steady increases. His enjoyment of everything Chinese was spontaneous, his gaiety infectious, his sense of humor bubbling over.

Ford admired everything Chinese: the architecture, the art. He liked the delicacy of Chinese paintings on rice paper and on silk, with their vast landscapes, their exquisite heads of animals and birds, the effect of perspective achieved by superimposing one object on top of another. But more than anything else in China, he loved her people with their attitude toward life, their quiet use of leisure. And he did everything possible to identify himself with the Chinese: the food he chose, the clothes he wore, his whole manner of living, all were Chinese. Father Mark Chai once said: "[His] love for China was so genuine that he appreciated the Chinese culture and customs better than most Chinese priests. He also interpreted many phases of the Chinese way of life better than we did." Once when a young missioner first arrived in Kaying, Ford, dressed in skull cap and long Chinese gown, went to the bus terminal to meet him. The new man failed to recognize his bishop because "Ford looked as much Chinese as any man in the place."

When Ford reflected on the pleasure he experienced being with the Chinese—or just being in China—he admitted, "the thrill had a touch of pain in it, in thinking that I found another people more appealing than my own. . . . Granted that America is all that enthusiasts claim for it, I still prefer our Chinese. This," he conceded, "may sound exaggerated to those brought up from childhood on the China of Gulliver's Travels. . . . The same press that has stereotyped our dress and speech has falsified our notions of the East and we look for nothing good from the bandit-ridden, topsy-turvy Orient of our imagination." Ford's Hak-ka Chinese were beyond reproach. "Whatever of China we write," he admitted, "we write not of all China or of every Chinese, we vouch simply for the Chinese under our eyes. There may be bad Chinese elsewhere," he conceded; "I don't know, or at least I am not discussing them. . . . There are, I suspect, some bad Chinese here too, but if I choose to close my eyes or wink at them it does not lessen my pleasure in the good Chinese I know."

His feeling for the Chinese people is exemplified in this excerpt from a letter he wrote to Maryknoll in 1937:

It is a fact that even missioners have a preference for certain peoples, though it need not affect their work at all; and in a group of missioners from different fields, although each will jealously defend his own adopted country, subrosa and wistfully they concede that the Chinese are "ace high," "the cream of the lot." I accept their estimate . . . and pass it on to you without remark, as I am a bit biased in the matter, laboring in Kwangtung, which all concede the best province in

China, and living with the Hak-kas, who are by many thought to be the finest in Kwangtung. . . .

My first reaction to close contact with the Chinese was the startling thought that Christianity has not a monopoly on virtue. In other words we are not working among a depraved, degraded race with atavistic tendencies little removed from vicious cannibalism. I knew this before I set foot on Chinese soil, but I discounted it and agreed, *a priori*, with the more common notion that pagan people could not be virtuous. . . . We, who were from childhood brought up as Christians, find it hard to realize the strength of natural virtues. . . .

The common life of the average Chinese is, to say the least, a remote preparation for Christian living. There is a firmness of character established by early rising, hard work . . . a resistance to softening tendencies, a tradition of sacrifice for family, a suppressing of self-seeking and a striving for the common good, a stoical acceptance of the inclemency of the weather, rough food and less than dainty clothing, all of which . . . eminently fit them for Christian ideals. . . . I think it is important in the day dreams of your future work not to underestimate the natural virtues of the Chinese. . . .

During the thirties, the Kaying mission made relatively good progress by means of a catechumenate system whereby persons interested in the doctrine were invited to the mission for a period of six weeks of intensive indoctrination after the rice was planted and later when it had been harvested. Not all of the Kaying Maryknollers were in accord with this type of catechesis and some objected to increasing the number of Christians by feeding prospective converts. Yet Ford knew that these same missioners had no alternative method by which to build up the mission. Through the catechumenates the number of adult converts rose appreciably. Here and there a well-to-do family and individual converts among the student class were brought into the Church, but for the most part, the catechumens were from among the poor. For this reason many intellectuals with some justification referred to them as "rice Christians." This did not in any way discourage Ford. He would raise his own elite. He would have his Christians spread the faith among their friends and relatives. A soul is a soul, he said, and in the eyes of God a beggar's soul is as precious as a mandarin's.

Neighboring missioners, observing the progress in Kaying, asked what the secret of Ford's success was—for the new Christians were zealous, well-instructed converts. The people themselves were a part of the answer, as was the grace of God, of course. But in no small measure, it was Ford himself. He directed his missioners to urge every Christian to take a part in spreading the gospel.

"Preach the gospel to every creature." This command of our Lord, Ford reasoned, demanded a personal response and a personal involvement. He wanted the Chinese Christians to be a dynamic, united, daily witness; through them God would speak to the world in its agony. "Tell everyone you meet," he would tell the new Christians at Confirmation time, "about the Light of the world, about the Lamb of God who takes away the sins of the world, about the Saviour of the world." Christians were to think not only of their own personal salvation, but of their neighbor's as well.

"Encourage the laity not only to live the faith, but to bring it to others," he instructed his priests, and urged them to let no Sunday pass without commenting in their sermons on the responsibility the Christians have to introduce their non-Christian neighbors to the Church. His missioners were to think of China not as a place containing potential church members, but rather as a part of the world needing a Saviour. His warning bears repeating: "If the world regards the Church as quite irrelevant, it is because we do not concern ourselves with the world and its problems."

Each year new missioners were assigned to Kaying by the superiors of the Maryknoll Fathers and Sisters. In 1931 an effort was made to have Father William Downs prepare a much-needed language course for the new missioners from the States. The Sisters, with their more orderly schedule, pursued the course conscientiously. However, because of the shortage of men, the new priest was sent almost immediately to one of the mission stations, where he was left to follow the program with the help of an older priest and a Chinese teacher. This was far from a satisfactory arrangement for learning a language as difficult as Chinese and it was surprising that the missioners spoke the tongue as well as they did.

Plans for the mission were reviewed frequently. New missions were opened annually; the work expanded constantly. For those who were working directly with Ford, it was interesting to watch the quiet, unobtrusive manner in which he was building up his mission. He never spoke or wrote his reprimands "at the top of his voice," as this typical passage written to one of the younger missioners illustrates. "I feel, after long experience in China, that what we lose out on is utilizing the ceremonies of the Church. We Americans are a bit free and easy about ritual. . . . The Chinese tend toward solemnity and in the Church services we have all the materials right at hand for quite elaborate ceremonies.

I mention this, frankly, as I sized you up as being a bit inclined to neglect this phase of the work."

Francis Ford was one of those leaders who distribute the load and thereby awaken initiative and touch unplumbed depths in subordinates who frequently go on to accomplish much good. He gave his men opportunities to learn and to mature so that their response to pressure would be seasoned by judgment and experience. He did not mind mistakes so long as the same mistake was not made twice. Certainly he did not wish to face the prospect of a severe discontinuity in the quality of leadership. His hand was firm when necessity required it, but normally, his hand was hidden. He wanted his fellow missioners to work in a tranquil atmosphere; he would urge them only to be alert to all opportunities and to keep busy. He could be approached at any time; he would talk unendingly about mission problems or about the Chinese, or for that matter, about anything under the sun. A delightful conversationalist, his talk, filled with common sense and uncommon sagacity, displayed a mind stacked with layer after layer of experience.

Although he stressed the principle that the missioners were in China primarily to establish the Church, still nothing pleased Ford more than a parish report that indicated a sharp increase in the number of Christians. Annually he compiled the statistics of the mission for his reports to Rome and to Maryknoll, and he was proud and pleased to observe the steady numerical growth. (By 1940 Kaying's original four thousand Catholics had increased to about twenty thousand.) The new Christians were not to sit back and "enjoy their Christianity." They were to be disturbed by and involved in the problems and needs of their fellow men. He tried to make the Christians mindful of the dignity that membership in the universal Church brought them.

His goal was not so much one of bringing people together in the Church, as it was of sending them as witnesses out to the world with a conviction of their mission. For this they needed constant visiting, constant encouraging.

Ford had no intention of minimizing the work of those missioners who carried on teaching assignments or who engaged in medical work. But for his Kaying mission, the time had not yet arrived for such emphasis. "We are here to preach the gospel," he reminded us. "We are not school teachers, or medical doctors, or philanthropists. My stand on charity may sound a bit hard-hearted and therefore un-Christian, but," he insisted, "the point is missed completely if such a conclusion is drawn. I have no quarrel with charitable works. I simply do not want our meager staff of missioners tied down to an institution, for the direction of which they are not qualified."

Nor did he have the funds for the construction of clinics, hospitals, or orphanages. In answer to criticisms of his policy on charities, he frequently presented the financial barrier; yet had he had the funds to dot China with hospitals and clinics and asylums, he would still have maintained that the missioners' aim should be to energize the people into establishing such institutions. His guideline was to "develop the responsibility for these works in the local people."

Actually there were a few economic programs started by Maryknollers in the Kaying mission and Ford made no objection. His policy was fixed, however. He enforced a strict policy that the projects should not involve the priest's personal direction and distract him from what Ford considered the priest's primary spiritual purpose. When Father James McCormick started a rice cooperative in Kaying, Ford approved the project, adding: "The Chinese people must take the lead. It must be their enterprise."

Another example that might be cited is the Rice Bank initiated by Father Maynard Murphy in his rural mission in the western part of the diocese. From the Rice Bank families could borrow rice at a small rate of interest instead of paying the usual exorbitant rates demanded by unscrupulous landowners and business men. Murphy introduced fruit and olive trees, as well as vegetable projects, to enlarge the meager diet. Futhermore, during the "off season" he helped to organize road building and other work to give employment to willing workers.

A Coat of Arms

The mission was growing; the missioners were getting results. Everyone seemed satisfied. Ford, in a letter to Maryknoll, reported: "In the decade which has passed, we find nothing spectacular in the development of the Kaying field, only an unswerving emphasis on the building up of a native Church."

Rome recognized the mission's progress. Early in the summer of 1935 a cable came to Kaying from Rome announcing that the mission had been raised from the status of a prefecture to that of a vicariate, and that the first bishop was to be Monsignor Francis X. Ford. Ford was not appointed the bishop of a diocese, in the canonical sense, for there were no dioceses in China at that time, but of a "vicariate apostolic" which was directly responsible to the Prefect of the Congregation of Propaganda in Rome. The creation of Vicars Apostolic (Vicars of the Pope) was a device begun in the seventeenth century for "mission countries" to evade legally the impasse of Pope Alexander VI's 1493 Bull of Demarcation by which the world outside of Europe was divided between Spain and Portugal. The papal decree gave the kings of each country the "right of patronage" which included the authority to appoint bishops in new dioceses.

With characteristic modesty and wit, the new bishop commented, on hearing the news, "It's going to be more difficult to dress from now on." And in a letter to Maryknoll he said: "My appointment as Vicar Apostolic of Kaying came last night. I was living in hopes that the Holy Ghost would come to the mission's rescue, but it looks as though even mediocre sanctity is not a *sine qua non*. I'm shy at making promises of reform, knowing my weaknesses, but fortunately the average holiness of the Kaying priests is high enough to stand against me, and I feel that God will not take it out on the rest of them to punish me."

It was his hope that Bishop James Anthony Walsh, the Superior General and co-founder of Maryknoll would consecrate him at Maryknoll. Ford said he hesitated to request him to perform the ceremony because Walsh at that time was not in good health. But on September 21, 1935, in the Maryknoll Sisters' Motherhouse chapel, Bishop Walsh performed the long impressive ceremony attended by twenty bishops and over two hundred priests: it was to be his last public function. Shortly before he died a few months later, Maryknoll's co-founder said of Francis Ford: "As we seek to define the outstanding trait of the mission career of this pioneer Maryknoller, we find it summed up in the simple statement that he identified himself in understanding love with this Chinese people."

For the motto on his episcopal coat of arms Ford chose the Latin word *"Condolere"* (to have compassion) from the fifth chapter of St. Paul's letter to the Hebrews. There could be no more fitting word placed across his episcopal shield: compassion. It was on the poor and afflicted he showered his compassion, loving them with an agony of pity for their poverty and their pain, caring for them with the same gentleness as he would have rendered to the suffering Body of Christ. *"Condolere,"* Father Drought remarked in his sermon; "he takes it as a promise; we interpret it as a triumph, the triumph of the compassionate Christ."

Certainly in China Ford could not forget his motto—there was so much to weep for: poverty, sickness, paganism. Ford saw China as a country constantly in travail to find its peace, constantly in travail to find its dignity. But what moved him most was the silence of his people in their misery. As he put it in a letter to Maryknoll, there is "no brooding or whining, just a dull stupor that does not even cry for food. They are beyond tears." At times, as he watched the never-ending struggle for mere existence, for a mouthful of food, he was filled with abhorrence at his people's condition and with frustration because of his inability to alleviate their predicament. "I would much prefer to feed the hungry," he said, "than to write about them, but when a Bishop's pocketbook is flat, and all available means are used up, and the eyes shrink from the gaunt spectres that haunt our doorway persistent in their hope of some relief, I must hide myself behind my analysis." He saw the problem of poverty and hunger in China as one still further aggravated by the lack of lines of communications. "There will still be famine from natural causes in a land where the staple crops are not diversified, but roads and railways would do much to counterbalance this. . . ."

Writing for the readers of Maryknoll's mission magazine, he gives a further description of poverty among the Chinese. "Here in China, poverty is a question of degree. It has never been considered a disgrace or a bar to local esteem, and the poor in a village may mingle with the rich without embarrassment, so little do fine clothes or a good table or external show affect relations in China." He observed that in his whole territory there was no exclusive club for the wealthy. The poor had free access to the social life of the village. They drank from the same teapot, smoked the common water pipe, shared the same fan, and contributed their shrewd comments to the conversation on a par with their neighbors. "Hence," he concluded, "it is difficult to distinguish in ordinary times between the moderately well-to-do and the poor, especially in the villages . . . It is only when famine strikes that poverty is clearly visible."

After the Bishop's return to Kaying, life went on much as it had before his consecration. Thinking of his fellow members of the hierarchy in Europe and America, Ford wrote: "The average bishop in America would envy us bishops in China, for even the most patient of them must hanker for a little of our informality and simplicity of life. To be treated like any other human being and pass whole days of travel unrecognized, or when recognized to be taken for granted without fuss; to have a seat on the bus depend on your elbows and not on your rank; to help push the bus up a steep grade, to be physically tired from a twenty mile walk . . . these are a few of the pleasures rarely possible for an American bishop."

Because he, himself, lived a simple, unpretentious life in an old Chinese farmhouse, without any visible comforts, no means of travel except public conveyances, trucks and sampans, he was as close to his people as it was physically possible for a foreigner to be. His episcopal office was a continual reminder that he who bears the mitre must offer sacrifices for his own sins, must feel compassion for the sufferings of others. Among the rich, Ford had no friends; they either ignored him or scorned him. And yet ironically enough, in the end he was forced into prison as a friend of the rich and an enemy of the poor.

To Ford's virtue of compassion must be added his humility. He bore his high office without arrogance, without any visible change in his attitude toward others. He deeply felt that he was made a bishop to serve. This represented for him the essence of his episcopacy. So accurately did it do so and so magnificently did he fulfill his ideal, that his authority was in evidence only when it was necessary. He wanted none of the outer wrappings of the episcopal office, none of the veneer. He constantly tried to put himself on the level of the rest of his missioners, speaking with great simplicity and always with a spontaneous outpouring of the heart.

On one occasion, he was walking away from the seminary following a conference of priests when a newly arrived missioner called him urgently from some distance: "Your Excellency, Your Excellency." Ford continued to converse with his companion unaware of the voice that repeatedly called him. As the young priest drew closer, Bishop Ford turned and asked, "Is he calling for me?" He stopped, waited for the priest and then said simply: "Look, young man, let's have no more of this 'Excellency' business over here." His missioners were to call him "Monsignor" and nothing else.

While Ford cared little for the external trappings of the episcopacy, he never forgot that he was the leader of the mission. When giving directions, or announcing a decision, his voice was unmistakably clear and assured. With patience he would hear out a difficult problem, listening until the man had finished and then calmly giving the solution. He never appeared surfeited, bored or blasé; he never tired discussing his work. Ford was completely involved in all the details of the mission. He was the director of activities, but never the sole dreamer of new ways, never the only planner of new projects. He was well aware that he could not by himself accomplish the smallest percentage of all that had to be done, so he would prepare and encourage others and thus multiply himself.

In Kaying Ford enjoyed few of the amenities of episcopal life. He was simply the shepherd of the flock. The very meaning of his responsibility as shepherd was for him to reassure, to encourage, to seek and to save what was lost. His authority was simply a mandate to serve and to bring all to the Truth. He never intended to rest with the few thousand Christians the French Fathers left him, nor was he ever content with the slowly increasing size of his flock. "Other sheep I have that are not of this fold, I must bring them also."

Father Bush

In the Hak-ka area there were relatively fewer bandits than there had been in Yeungkong. For several years conditions had been so comparatively tranquil that Ford in a letter to Maryknoll wrote: "I've been glorying over much in the peacefulness of this new mission . . . I look forward to a natural death in peace."

However, even his beloved Hak-ka hills were not entirely free of bandits. The few years of peace that followed the Communist attacks on the Kaying mission were interrupted by a series of bandit raids due in large part to two successive crop failures.

On the twenty-eighth of April in 1935, Father Henry Bush left his mission at Shakchin to say Mass in a village about ten miles away. The following day he began his return journey, accompanied by his house boy and his dog. Somewhere along the mountain paths, bandits captured him. Ford wrote to Maryknoll, "That was the last trace we have of him. Happily, Father Bush has a good command of the language, is in excellent health and has a strong stomach that can stand prolonged rough fare; he is neither impulsive nor nervous and can be counted on to meet the situation calmly."

Ford immediately notified the American consul in Swatow, who passed the word along to the American minister in Peiping. Nanking was contacted and the Chinese authorities were told that they must assume full responsibility for the safe delivery of Father Bush. Possibly a thousand Chinese Nationalist troops were dispatched to the area where Bush was last seen. They gradually narrowed the field by destroying possible hiding places and by watching anyone who sold rice or salt to strangers in any large quantities. Thus deprived of adequate food and kept constantly on the run within an ever narrowing area, the bandits finally decided to break through the encirclement. Twenty bandits were killed and twenty others, along with Bush, were captured.

Tears of joy and gratitude filled Father Bush's eyes when the Nationalist soldiers released his arms and freed him. Taken to the American Consulate in Canton, he was given a good meal, after which he was put on the Canton-Kowloon train for a rest in Hong Kong.

No ransom was offered at any time during the weeks Bush was held. Ford remarked, however, that he had to pay "about two hundred dollars for the consul's travel expenses and for telegrams . . . and there is still a big item for banquets for the soldiers after Father Bush returns here." Ford was warm in his expression of gratitude to members of the U.S. State Department, particularly a young consular official named Everett Drumright, who later became United States Ambassador to China. Consul Hinke of Swatow and Consul General Spiker of Canton were also given special praise for "dropping every other business to concentrate on the case."

The importance of Father Bush's experience in Bishop Ford's history lay in the contacts that the Bishop made at that time with the American State Department officials in China and with the legitimate Chinese Nationalist Government officials in Nanking and Canton. Ford kept a record of his letters and telegrams to these people, along with copies of the replies from the United States and Chinese authorities. It was this file, more than anything else, that later gave the Communists the "proof" that Ford was an agent of the imperialist American government.

 # CHAPTER VI

CONFUCIUS

With coarse food to eat, water for drink and a bent
elbow for a pillow—even in such a state I could
be happy. As for wealth and honor obtained by improper
means, they are like the fleeting cloud to me.
   The Basic Teaching of Confucius, MILES DAWSON, page 47

JESUS CHRIST

The foxes have dens, and the birds of the air have
nests; but the Son of Man has nowhere to lay his head.
                                        MATTHEW 8:20

War

   During the nineteen thirties Japan was consolidating
and expanding her military and political gains in China.
She created a puppet regime called Manchukuo early in
1932, consisting of Manchuria combined with Jehol. In 1933,
Japan drove the Nationalist soldiers out of eastern Hopei
province where another puppet government was set up.

   While Japan was ruthlessly carrying out her "mission
in East Asia," Chiang Kai-shek continued to appease the
Japanese stalling for time in an attempt to unify the country and train a modern army, for he knew—despite the
strong sentiment among the young people to challenge the

Japanese at once—he had no military force with which to face Japan's armed might.

Russia, to relieve any Japanese pressure on herself, encouraged China to fight. Communist propaganda agitated for immediate Chinese armed resistance against Japan. Among the professional classes, the anti-Japanese National Salvation Association was formed. On university campuses, the students' National Salvation Union sprang up. Though incited by the Communists, these were genuine patriotic movements. There seemed to be in 1934 a uniform mandate for Chiang to fight the Japanese without further delay.

This insistence embarrassed Chiang. He realized that resistance was hopeless until China became militarily stronger. But there was another policy consideration that influenced his decision to delay. Chiang wanted first to effect the unification of the country, and for him that meant the extinction of the Communists.

The Communists who survived the abortive coup in Kaying in 1928 had retreated to the sheltered mountainous area of Kiangsi province. Here they gathered support from discontented peasants, recruited an army, and set up a program of agrarian reforms. They drove out the Kuomintang officials, dispossessed rich landlords, and divided the land. In 1931, in the Kiangsi hills, the Chinese Soviet Republic was proclaimed with Mao Tse-tung at its head; the next year—appreciating the popular sentiment—it declared war on Japan!

Chiang was forced to act, not against the Japanese, but against the Communists. He made a tenuous truce with Japan in 1933 and turned his strength on Mao Tse-tung's forces in the south. His military offensive against the better-trained Communist guerillas was unsuccessful, but a force of about three hundred thousand Nationalists finally succeeded in surrounding the Communists in the Kiangsi and

Fukien areas and cutting off their food supply. Desperately short of food and material, eighty thousand Communists broke through the encirclement and started the legendary Long March to Yenan in Shensi province in the northwest. Only twenty thousand reached the destination a year later, in the fall of 1935. It was here at Yenan that Mao Tse-tung, Chou En-lai, and Chu Teh, master tacticians, reorganized the Chinese Reds and began recruitment for a campaign to take over the whole of China.

On July 7, 1937, Japan attacked some Chinese troops at the Marco Polo Bridge on the outskirt of Peking. With little opposition the city fell to the Japanese, who took Tientsin a few days later. Shanghai was next. There Chinese resistance stiffened and the Japanese suffered severe losses before capturing the important port city. Then, on December 12, the American gunboat "Panay" was sunk. This was followed by the infamous "rape of Nanking." Despite the repugnant feeling of the world, no Western power was willing to come to China's aid. The Nationalist government decided to continue its resistance on its own.

Brushing aside the obvious fact that they were militarily unable to cope with the modern Japanese military machine, Chinese students called for Chiang Kai-shek's resignation. Nationalistic fervor was mounting; an aroused patriotism had reached a climax. Chiang had no other course but to resist. "If China as a nation has to be terminated," he declared, "let it be terminated by a war rather than by continuous defeat." That was the popular sentiment. "We will fight to the bitter end," he promised, "no matter what the sacrifices. . . . What Japan has done to us cannot be tolerated by a nation with self-respect." Overnight there was a national unity such as had never been seen before in China's history. Even warlords and Communist leaders joined the resistance.

This decision did not mean, however, that there was domestic accord in China. There was considerable dissension within the Kuomintang Party, as evidenced by the shocking defection of Wang Ching-wei, who in 1940 became the puppet heading the government Japan set up in Nanking.

In addition to the continual bombing of their cities, the Chinese were confronted with another demoralizing factor, inflation. At one point one United States dollar could purchase more than ten thousand dollars of worthless Chinese paper money. Unscrupulous hoarding by the favored few increased the domestic discontent. At harvest time rice was bought cheaply and sold later at mercilessly high prices. That the rich were getting richer and the poor, poorer was one of the charges the Communists made against the Nationalist government, which, they claimed, did nothing to protect the peasants.

Internal deterioration during the war years was further aggravated by the growing strength of the Chinese Communists, who were extending their authority as their guerillas went along. Nationalist and Communist armies worked together in a few engagements against the Japanese until 1941 when an order issued by Chiang was either misunderstood or ignored by the Communists. The Nationalists opened fire and forced the Communists to retreat to the northwest. Like all Gaul, the country was now divided into three parts: Japanese-occupied China, Free China, and Communist China.

Courage and Sacrifices at Kaying

Throughout the late thirties, Kaying and the larger towns in the Hak-ka mission were subject to continual bombings by Japanese war planes. There were a few military objectives in the area—such as the bridge spanning the Mei River, a few troops, and some supplies in transit. Although these objectives might call for an occasional air attack, the purpose of the daily pounding seemed to be simply harassment and intimidation of the people. To reassure his superior at Maryknoll, Ford predicted that "even with the imminent occupation of Swatow, I do not think we shall see much of the war firsthand, as we are off the beaten path somewhat and Japanese troop movements avoid our mountains." And this turned out to be substantially true: the Kaying mission, situated in the northern part of Kwangtung province, was never occupied by the Japanese, though they did on occasion cross through the southern section of Ford's territory.

But twice a day the bass-viol drone of the twin engine bombers could be heard as they approached to attack one of the defenseless towns. They would leisurely line up their target and unload their hissing shower of death. How the missioners dreaded that ominous monotone moaning against the high blue sky! The best they could do if there were no time to run out into the country was to lie flat and listen to the whistle of the bombs, praying to hear the thunderous explosion—a sign that they were still alive. Not until Pearl Harbor and Hong Kong were attacked, and America and Britain were drawn into the Pacific War, did the attacks on the unprotected towns abate.

During the air attacks by the Japanese planes, Bishop Ford was the one person who showed no outward sign of anxiety. Courage, of course, is a private matter, yet it is a contagious matter too. Whether it was bandits or bombings, loneliness or the daily demands on his patience, Ford, at least externally, met each challenge quietly, without fanfare. He always seemed able to generate that extra courage needed when crises arose. Each incident strengthened him to endure more, and prepared him for the coming ordeal of imprisonment and death. He could write in 1941: "War has its purifying element, not only that resulting from pain and misery shared with others, but also that from lighter moments shared in common. In every dreadful incident, there is usually some comical mishap that relieves the strain and irons out the anxious lines on every face. This is especially good for us Westerners in China who have a tendency to solemnity and aloofness and who lack the natural simplicity of the average Chinese crowd.

"We like to think," he wrote, "that our restraint betokens coolness under fire and a calmness in emergencies. Where others shout, we stolidly smoke our pipes; where others wave their arms and point out the approaching airplanes, we content ourselves with a squinting glance and a grim appraisal of its direction and speed. While others frantically run in all directions, we uphold our pride by sauntering, content with our estimation of ourselves. . . ."

One day, having sufficient warning to leave his house near the bridge, he hastened out into the country and approached a shelter dug for four, already crowded with ten people. Seeing the Bishop, they generously pressed themselves together, as only Chinese peasants can, and let him squeeze in. The roof was built for much shorter occupants. "To stand upright," he wrote, "would be to lose your head, so you add the final touch by attempting to squat in the Chinese manner."

Ford often referred to the sudden curious silence that followed the terrifying blast of the bombs.

It stills all natural life and drives off introspection. You become conscious, in a detached sort of way, of the centipedes and other insects shaken from the roof and sides of the dugout. You peek out the doorway and notice how green the rice fields are and how bright is the sun; the hush of the frogs, and birds, and crickets is startling for the moment. . . . Then you glance at your fellow cave men and suddenly grin, thinking of the sight you must present to them, disheveled and dirty. As though this gave permission, they release their fright and unleash an outburst of laughter. Your answering smile becomes a chuckle, then a full-blown laugh, and soon the whole dugout echoes and melts the sounds until you are one with the group. Laughter levels as surely as a bomb. As all scramble for the light and slowly meander home, you feel close to the people and understand them a bit better.

What was most amazing during the air raids was the constant buoyancy of the Bishop. He continued to move spryly, smile evenly, and speak calmly and wisely. "Confidence in God," he once said in a conference, "is a necessary missionary virtue, not only in times of crisis, but at all times." When one of the missioners suggested moving the mission temporarily out into the country, or at least to send the Sisters into the mountains away from their dangerous proximity to a vulnerable bridge, Ford insisted the Japanese would not bomb the mission, nor the Sisters' convent. A short time later, however, he did reluctantly agree to send the Sisters to a safer place.

As the world tension increased and the possibility of American involvement in the conflict became more imminent, the American consul in Swatow requested that Ford withdraw himself and all Maryknoll missioners from the Kaying area and return to the United States. The final of three warnings came in late October of 1941. The consul stated that the United States government would take no responsibility for the safety of the Maryknollers in the area if they did not leave the mission within two weeks. Ford replied that he did not hold the consul or the American government in any way responsible for their safety and that all Maryknollers would remain at their missions. Six weeks after the consul's final warning, Japan attacked Hong Kong and Pearl Harbor.

Once the United States was drawn into the Pacific War, the Kaying mission was cut off from all contact with the outside. Writing to his missioners at that time, Bishop Ford said with typical understatement: "We must anticipate a few lean years," adding, "for which, of course, there need be no complaints." For several years the mission had been showing steady progress and he expected the progress to continue. However, following American involvement in the Asiatic conflict, new missioners ceased to arrive. Chinese priests ordained in Rome and Hong Kong could not return to Kaying. There was a noticeable decline in the number of new Christians. And remittance of funds from Maryknoll came to a halt.

"Money is not the *sine qua non* for converts," said Ford at this time, "but it is necessary for catechists' salary if new converts are to receive adequate instruction for Baptism." Appraising the situation philosophically, he said, "It certainly can test our patience and initiative, while we carry on without the aids to which we have been accustomed."

Ford asked every missioner to cooperate in cutting expenses to the minimum. Paid catechists and teachers had to be discharged. Those priests who had motorcycles, cameras, or typewriters were able to sell them to wealthy Chinese refugees from Hong Kong and Canton who were seeking shelter in their ancestors' homes in the Hak-ka hills.

They desired to invest their ridiculously inflated Chinese currency into goods that could be redeemed at the end of the war. Through these sales the mission was maintained, but at a much reduced pace. The priests gradually became accustomed to doing without such items as meat, coffee, American tobacco, and other such luxuries they had formerly thought to be necessities.

A rewarding experience of the war years was the generous way in which the Chinese Christians responded to the needs of the mission personnel. They supplied them with rice and eggs and an occasional chicken, gifts that were costly sacrifices from people who had barely enough for their own tables. But in that way, the Christians demonstrated that they could be relied upon in an emergency. Those who contributed little or nothing to the Church in normal times now saw that their help was needed. As Bishop Ford put it, "their sacrifices have heartened and comforted us."

Hunger

As life became intolerable in the Japanese-occupied area, Kaying became a haven for refugees. Carrying all their worldly possessions on their back, driving before them a precious water buffalo or pig, they were the epitome of destitution. Bishop Ford commented, "It needs a stout heart to walk through the streets of the city these days." As the unhappy, unwanted, hopeless hundreds ringed the city with slums, the Kaying missioners could see an explosive potential building up. Here among the human huddles was the incubator of revolution.

The Chinese Government, through the National Relief Association, did accomplish something for the relief of air raid victims: Madame Chiang Kai-shek's National Refugee Children's Association did help many war orphans. But the problem was far greater than the limited funds available could solve. After Pearl Harbor, when funds from America were cut off, missioners tried to help the war victims by sending local church committees to shop-keepers in the towns to solicit rice and to the local officials for funds. Also, they set up a small industrial school on the mission property where youngsters learned to make fans, baskets, and other useful articles from bamboo, which were sold to the shops in Kaying. But the missioners were able to assist only a small percentage of those in need.

In 1944, the United Nations Relief and Rehabilitation Administration was established through an agreement signed in Washington by representatives of forty-four nations. Its purpose was to "plan and administer measures for the relief of victims of war" in any area under the control of the signatory nations.

UNRRA help reached the Kaying mission via Chung-king, the provisional Chinese capital. An area branch, called the Kwangtung International Relief Committee, was formed to handle the UNRRA funds. Bishop Ford was appointed chairman and Maryknoll Sister Joan Marie was named secretary of the committee formed by a representa-tive of the mayor, a Baptist missionary, a Lutheran doctor, and the author of this book. The relief money was divided between Protestant and Catholic groups, and rice, salt, and oil were purchased in Kaying. A temporary kitchen super-vised by the Sisters was set up in the mission where rice gruel was prepared. For many refugees their only sustenance was the bowl of rice gruel they came for daily: occasionally as many as four thousand refugees were fed at the kitchen each day. (Nevertheless, young Communists would come to harangue those waiting in the rice line and to impugn the motives of the missioners and of the United States.) By the time UNRRA ended in 1947, over a half billion dollar's worth of food and supplies had been sent to China.

Those at the mission marveled at the refugees' outward stoic acceptance of suffering and privation. Stamina to endure was inbred in the Chinese through generations of hard living. Except for the very few, from birth to death, all conformed to a severe regime. There was a spartan simplicity in their home life, a monastic plainness in the home's furnishings, no frills, nor frippery. They learned to enjoy life in human companionship, not in incidentals. The refugees that poured into Kaying bearing their sorrows, could still show an incredible smile, an apparent nonchalance in their pain, an endurance unconscious of heroism, an impersonal, unselfish fatalistic outlook on life. The sadness in their faces came from the knowledge that they had no food to give their children when they awoke hungry.

To add disaster to an already critical food shortage, in 1943 there was a failure of the sweet potato crop. Rice from Southeast Asia had been cut off by the Japanese occupation. Bishop Ford sent Father Henry Madigan to Chungking in an effort to get help for the stricken area. The famine was so severe that people were bartering furniture and clothing for a few pounds of rice for their families. This was not the lot of the few, but the fate of the majority. Countless numbers died of starvation. Hunger was a giant agony. People mixed the leaves of trees with the chaff from the rice threshings, and cooked the concoction for their daily sustenance. Others dug up tree roots in the mountains and pounded them into a paste which they cooked. About so much inequality, so much poverty, no missioner could be unconcerned. There were days when the relief funds were exhausted and refugees had to be turned away with empty bowls. These were the saddest hours.

Neighboring missions staffed by Italian and German missioners were practically at a standstill. Since they were nationals of the Axis countries at war with China, their missioners were interned for the duration. Despite the fact that some of his own men were ill and the Kaying mission was understaffed, Ford sent two Maryknollers to take over parishes in the Hoifong area where the Italian missioners from Milan had been working. In his instructions to one of the men, Father Howard Trube, Ford wrote: "We realize that this sudden assignment is as hard as it is unexpected . . . but I am sure you will understand the situation and cooperate fully. . . . Stay in the smaller parishes, off the beaten path, for the time being. I do not fear any big movement of troops your way, but on general principle if it appears that trouble is coming, it would be more prudent to retreat to some smaller inland parish out of the line of the main routes until things settle down. I mention this as there is no sense in endangering your usefulness by being interned when prudence would outwit the move."

The Bishop assured the Maryknollers working outside the Kaying territory that they were frequently in his thoughts: "I dare say there is not a day goes by without several hours of daydreaming about all of you. Much of my daydreaming, I must admit, is self-pity; I was not built to sit at a typewriter all day and deal with bookkeeping details or official reports, and I'd give my shirt (or episcopal ring) any day to get out in parish work." This was one of Ford's characteristic understatements. Actually, despite the difficulties of wartime travel, he continued to visit his missioners in remote areas and to administer the details of his territory.

At the Hostel

In 1940, the Kaying church occupied a sprawling old Chinese farmhouse across the river from the city of Kaying. One third of the house continued to be occupied by the Wong family, the non-Christian owners. It was a place of no distinct design or period: a place that had been lived in and added to by successive generations of Wongs. As is characteristic of such dwellings in this area of China many small rooms had been added as the family increased and multiplied. Sons and grandsons did not move out to set up their own households after marriage; they raised their families in the ancestral home. However, as occasionally happens, the Wong family at the beginning of the present century started to decline; lack of sons left most of the home empty.

Bishop Ford occupied a small section of the Wong house where he had a few spare rooms for missioners who came in once a month or so to visit him on business.

Early in 1943, Bishop Ford moved from the Wong house to another farmhouse about three hundred yards away on the same side of the river. This large house was being used by the mission as a hostel for middle school boys. The war had brought about an acute shortage of priests, and because he was always willing to fill in where he was needed, Ford announced that he would live there and take over the direction of the Aquinas Hostel with its thirty-eight student residents. None of his men could say of him: upstream we did the rowing; downstream he poled the boat. "I hate just being bishop," he said. But there was more to it than the desire to be "doing something." Ford admired the Chinese students, and as director of the hostel it was possible for him to mix with them and be in an environment he loved.

If the Bishop assumed the directorship of the hostel primarily because he enjoyed the company of the students, he had yet a further motive. He wanted to win these future leaders to Christ and to learn from them all he could about China. "Old men are not always the wisest, and old ways are not always the best ways," he said.

Ford had frequently expressed an understanding and an appreciation of the important role the student plays in Chinese society. "In China, more than in the Western world," he said, "the student class reflects and voices the sentiments of the nation, and in China more than in most places, because the students have no antecedents, there is independence in their utterances. We in Kaying are in unusually close touch with the student class. This city is what we would call a 'college town' due to the predominance of its educational institutions, and it gives an index of the intellectual attitudes of the nation. Yet among the students we find a surprising seriousness in the viewpoint, a sturdy low pitch and cool unrhetorical appraisal of conditions; more reassuring still, we sense the recognition of moral values, the change from callow youth to clean manhood."

The Kaying mission had no Catholic high schools and Ford announced no plans for erecting one: first of all, because he felt there were enough government schools, and secondly, because he had not the funds to construct or support such institutions. However, he felt that Catholic boys from the outlying districts attending government schools in Kaying and other large towns should live in the Christian atmosphere of a Church-sponsored hostel. In the Kaying hostel there were rooms set aside for the chapel and for the bishop's office. The students crowded into the small bedrooms.

The Chinese students of the thirties and forties were a hard-working group. Their classes began early in the morning, many were at their books until late at night; and they gave the impression of being serious, nose-to-the-grindstone sort of youngsters. They were given a broad academic menu with a number of side dishes into which they might dip if they chose. For the most part they partook of this academic meal in buildings unattractive, unfunctional, and understaffed. And in their homes or hostels they digested the matter in poorly lit, poorly aired, and poorly furnished bedrooms.

Perhaps it would be wrong to say these students were rudderless, but it would not be wrong to say they were hungry for direction, for positive dedicated leadership, for a decisive voice calling the signals. During these years, the students appeared to be drifting along a stream of existence they knew was about to change its course. They awaited masters who would do what their elders could no longer do: teach them how to live together in peace, in justice, and in freedom.

Ford enjoyed talking about his students and in his reports to Maryknoll he frequently wrote about them. The sacrifice poor Chinese parents made to give their children an opportunity to study impressed him deeply. The difficulties the students endured compared to the average American youngsters also moved him. Each student was on his own from the moment he left home. Leaving his village for the first time, he took his own bedding, lamp, and oil and made his own arrangements for lodging. He cooked his own meals, washed his own clothes, made his own decisions. As a result, the Chinese high school student, in many respects, had a maturity comparable to a college student elsewhere.

The Chinese boys living in the hostel bought their own food, worked out their own schedule of study and play, disciplined themselves to regular hours, rose before dawn, and carefully set their room in order before starting off at about six o'clock for school, frequently without breakfast. The wartime schedule left the hours from ten in the morning to three in the afternoon free of classes because of the danger from air attack. Back at the hostel at ten, they prepared their first meal of the day. It might be seven in the evening before they were able to eat again. The rice and vegetable supper was followed by a brief period of recreation, then back to their little oil lamps and their books.

Some may think that all this independence would make the Chinese boy unruly. "But," explained Ford, always defending the youngsters he loved, "experience proves that as the Chinese boy grows up, he has a sedateness and a natural sturdiness not found in the average Western young man. This," observed Ford, "makes him a bit conservative, not sensitive to criticism; he is reticent and cautious about anything beyond the range of boyish naturalism. Thus he remains refreshingly youthful. Formality never tends to ostentation, but rather to simplicity and neatness."

Ford had a doting father's attitude toward his boys. Although the middle school students occasionally annoyed some of the missioners by taunting "foreign devil" at them, or by ridiculing their Chinese pronunciation, as far as Ford was concerned the students could do no wrong. They amazed him with their knowledge of trees and animals and creeping things, the texture of the soil, and the significance of the clouds.

Chinese youngsters were brought up to face the world of reality. Their parents felt that the sooner they acted like adults the better. Rather than developing a world of their own, as American children do, the Chinese early in life unobstrusively entered the world of adults. Chinese youngsters, living in the same house with their paternal grandparents and the families of their uncles and aunts, were not the exclusive rights of their parents, as they are in America. In China there was a pattern of mutual dependence between parents and children which welcomed the child's progress toward adulthood. The Chinese lad was not easily shocked by injustices, slights, or untruths. He was conditioned to expect these.

The young Chinese preferred to pause now and then rather than exert himself when it was not necessary to do so. He liked to enjoy what he had. Ford, thinking the students did not push themselves enough, that they were content with the status quo, would, in his talks to the hostel boys, try to make them feel an obligation to strive forward, to do better, to exert themselves. He would remind his students that scholarship, not wealth was the most important of commodities. They were not entirely convinced, having heard that in the United States it was wealth, not scholarship, that commanded prestige. Still the Chinese student was quite aware that his education gave him standing in his village. The middle school student in most cases knew there was not likely to be anyone in his region as highly educated as he. To acquire a good education was then more than a personal or family obligation; it was a clan responsibility as well. If he were so inclined, he could enter the literary-bureaucratic class, and the others in the village would defer to him obsequiously in speech and contact. The student knew that he could always return to his village. An old Chinese adage encouraged this: "Not to the big city to make it big, but to your home village repair, for it is folly to wear silk where no one will care." Yet, even if he failed, he knew he would never lose his place in the secure roots of the primary group—his family.

It is important to observe here that the pursuit of

knowledge in schools away from the village and the family, even in the 1930's was beginning to weaken the influence of the home. Ford referred to this in a letter to Maryknoll in 1943. "The new generation has learned to stand alone," he said, "and there may be a complete break with the traditional respect for parents and for village life."

All during the war years, Ford continued to direct the young students. He would teach English to the boys at night and help those who were having difficulty with their mathematics as he had done years ago at Cathedral College.

It was his intention to challenge the students, not only scholastically and politically, not only materially, but spiritually in terms of morality. He would impart a spirit other than the spirit of efficiency—something deeper, more lasting. He would impart the spirit of integrity, of purity, the spirit of patient suffering, of love and trust and the seeking for the truth, the spirit of freedom, of joy and humor. The Bishop wanted to create in his hostel a climate of good will wherein the students could see within themselves their capacity for achievement and wherein he could speak to them freely about Jesus Christ. He could not love these young men without sharing with them the joy of the gospel.

The tutor role that Ford assumed was consistent with his democratic, casual attitude toward his episcopal office. And in a sense, it was typically American also insofar as Americans feel that a leader's appeal is founded on actual contact with his fellowmen. By contrast the traditional Chinese official felt the wider his distance from the people, the higher his prestige. A Chinese dignitary had little desire to show himself to the public or to mix with the people. Bishop Ford would never insist on the dignity of his office. He wanted as little pomp and ceremony as possible. Though his attitude was contrary to the Chinese cultural pattern, the students in his hostel accepted him on his terms. As he put it: "Mitre and pectoral cross are out of sight; I am on my own as a man."

Not all of his hostel students remained loyal even during the forties; some left because they disliked the religious atmosphere; some left because they disliked the simple house rules. Yet Ford would remain cheerful even after ten thousand disappointments, affectionate and genial amid the thousands of interruptions and distractions. His consolation and peace rested in the love and service of his Master, for he aimed at His approval far more than the esteem of men. That does not mean that he did not look for the approval of men. He did. He loved those students not only for the sake of Christ, but for their own sake as well. He had an empathy with them that few of his missioners ever realized. He felt with them and for them and for their families; he was interested in everything they did . . . "rejoicing with them that rejoice, weeping with them that weep." In the eyes of his students, Ford was the least magisterial of all their teachers, the gentlest and most amiable of all their superiors.

Ford had visions of his hostel boys exerting a strong Christian influence in their schools and later in public life. The conversion of these young men, he felt, was an essential precondition of any lasting establishment of Christianity in China. In 1943 he wrote: "Since October . . . twelve pagan students were baptized and one of them surprised me last Sunday by announcing that his whole family wanted to go under instruction. The good Lord tempers my desk work with real gifts like that every so often. Incidentally, dealing with boys from seven different middle schools I've been told by several that they were approached by other students to join the Communist group."

This rather startling observation apparently had very little impact on Bishop Ford. Even when two Communist professors were executed on the school grounds because they failed to heed the government's warning against propagating the Marxist doctrine, Ford was inclined to regard the incident as an isolated case and to consider the Communist influence of no serious moment. He was confident that the Chinese would never accept a system that was materialistic, collectivistic, and anti-family. Like so many others, he discounted the Communist strength, their hatred, their determination.

Seeds on the Wind

Although the people at the mission saw very little of the Japanese after the attack on Pearl Harbor, they did have some contact with United States military personnel from time to time. American air men, flying from bases in west China, were occasionally downed by the Japanese in occupied eastern Kwangtung. Chinese guerillas frequently rescued them and brought them through Kaying on their way west. The pilots were always taken to the mission where they were given some clean clothing and a good meal and would in turn give the missioners the latest news of America, bringing them up to date on World War II slang.

In October of 1944, a group of United States Army engineers came to Kaying by jeep from the Kiangsi air base. Working out of Kaying until late in November, they operated as closely as possible to the Japanese-occupied areas around Swatow and Canton. It seemed quite normal and natural for the missioners to treat the soldiers with hospitality: indeed, after two years of isolation, the missioners were delighted to see people recently arrived from the United States. And apparently the Chinese accepted whatever contact the missioners had with their countrymen as quite proper. Certainly there was never a hint that the Maryknollers might be suspected of working in any capacity with the United States military forces.

After the engineers departed, the people in Kaying had no further contact with any branch of the United States armed forces until February 1945, when the Navy sent in teams to work with Chinese weather units. Frequently referred to as the "sampan" or "rickshaw" navy, the combined group was called SACO (Sino-American Cooperation Organization). They installed a large generator and radio sending station at Kaying to relay weather conditions and other information to the United States air bases in western China, from whence American ships at sea would be informed. Usually the scouting parties consisted of three persons: a United States Navy man, a Chinese military man, and a university student who would serve as interpreter. These small teams were frequently able to get behind Japanese lines.

On the whole, there seemed to be cordial relations between Chinese and American militarymen. However, there was some resentment toward U.S. military personnel on the part of the Chinese university students. A few Americans behaved with insufferable arrogance toward their interpreters and treated them as coolies. This was not entirely the fault of the individual G.I.: his school textbooks had taught him little about Chinese civilization and his own knowledge might not extend beyond opium, firecrackers, and chop suey. What the schools neglected to do the army could not provide: the orientation given the G.I. before he was sent to China was necessarily rushed and superficial. G.I.'s felt the Chinese did "everything backwards" because they wrote in columns from bottom to top, and from right to left, and because their books "start at the back and go forward." The Chinese felt precisely the same about them —Americans were the ones doing everything backwards. U.S. military personnel would remark on the Chinese "wolfing" their food with chopsticks, and the Chinese, who consider it bad manners to touch food with the hands once it is placed on the table, would express disgust at seeing Americans seize bread, break it apart, and convey it to their mouths with their hands.

Occasionally American military men would discuss international affairs with members of the mission and with the student interpreters. The Chinese students had learned about Columbus, Washington, Lincoln, and Benjamin Franklin, but the Americans knew little about the leading philosophers or literary figures of Asia. The Americans frequently found the students obstinate and unsympathetic toward their point of view and this frustrated them. As Americans, they were anxious to be accepted, to please, to leave a good image, to rate high on the pollster's world opinion. Not all the soldiers were condescending—nor did that attitude apply to the Navy personnel—but too many carried with them the conviction that there was no place on earth that could have anything better than the U.S.A. and no people could do anything better than Americans.

Such misunderstanding aside, there seemed to be no reason at the time to suspect that the Chinese would object to the missioners' association with their compatriots in the armed forces. The American military personnel worked closely with Chinese military: both groups shared the same goal—the eventual defeat of Japan.

It was not until that goal had been achieved that rumors reached the mission, early in 1946, that some middle school teachers had linked the priests directly with the intelligence activities of the United States government. They pointed to the missioners' association with the American units during the war.

At the time, Bishop Ford thought the accusation too absurd to be taken seriously.

Failing Health

Over the years, the demanding duties of missioner, mission superior, and bishop had required exceptional physical stamina; and for most of his life Ford had enjoyed rather good health. There was a toughness about him in the sense of being able to endure. Physically he was lean, although he engaged in no exercise except walking. Early in 1939, however, he began to complain of stomach pains. A Swiss medical missioner at the Kaying Lutheran hospital diagnosed the problem as a slight case of sprue, a most damaging tropical disease that causes chronic diarrhea and other digestive disturbances. Unable to get the proper rest and medical treatment and, later, proper food, the Bishop fought ill health all during the war, carrying on his many projects and duties with characteristic good cheer. He even cautioned his missioners about their own health, warning them not to overdo in the hot weather and making it a rule of the mission that no Maryknoller was to be exposed to the sun for more than an hour without either sun helmet or umbrella. "We Americans," he wrote to Father Trube, "have been so badly sold on the California ads about the value of sunshine, that we are apt to discount the difference between the mild U.S. sun and the peculiarly penetrating poison of the tropical brand."

He also exhorted his missioners to be careful about the food they ate. The Bishop told Trube in a letter written to Hoifong to try to buy some meat a couple of times a week even if it meant using money he felt should be used for some other purpose. As Ford put it, "The extra cost of good food is worth more to the Society than a doctor's bill." The Bishop, however, did not concern himself about his own food. "If [the cook] will keep the table relatively free from ants, I'll be satisfied," he remarked. Breakfast (after the Chinese manner) was his "big meal," for which he usually tried to get a bit of ham and some eggs. His lunch was a sweet potato and another egg; in the evening he would have rice gruel and toast. With such spartan fare he was quite happy, quipping that at least he didn't have to concern himself with excess weight or calories.

His consumption of tobacco was enormous. In his discussions his pipe was indicative of his mood. When he was on top of his subject he would repeatedly poke the stem at his victim, forcing home his points as he went along; in a thoughtful moment or in a crisis he would suck it, glaring over the bowl out into space. Sometimes he seemed to address his remarks to it as he refilled it. At other times he drew on the stem as though extracting ideas from it. Refilling the bowl of the pipe was a ritual he never altered. He would pour some tobacco into the palm of his left hand and stuff the bowl with his right index finger. Next he would blow his breath on the damp sulphur of the match-head and on the sandpaper side of the matchbox, then strike the match several times until it would ignite. Finally, with the closed matchbox he would press down the over-stuffed bowl and apply a second match to insure good burning. As he pulled on the stem, the curling smoke, the burning ash, the thick aroma gave him obvious satisfaction.

During the war years, he was forced to change from imported American pipe tobacco to the uncured, bitter, local product. He became so accustomed to the strong domestic brand that he carried a large supply of it back to the States when he returned to Maryknoll in 1946. However, his missioners were quick to observe that he had changed back to American tobacco while in the States and had brought back a good quantity when he returned to Kaying the following year.

Bishop Ford's health was not aided by the bitter cold which he dreaded. The Chinese houses he had rented were unheated, and when the temperature of the damp, rainy winter days dropped into the forties, he was quite uncomfortable. He would retreat to his bed as early as he could after freeing himself from his responsibilities to the hostel boys. There, under a blanket and a heavy Chinese quilt, with a heavy woolen stocking cap pulled down over his ears, he read by the light of a homemade camphor lamp. The room he occupied in the hostel was utterly devoid of any modern convenience (he used the same outdoor toilet facilities as the students); he lived in apostolic simplicity. On the walls of his room there were no soft paintings on silk, much as he admired them; there were no pictures at all on the gray adobe walls, only the crucifix over his bed; there were no distractions save his books piled on several boxes and on a corner table. Newman sat on the same chair with Cram, Chesterton, Fortescue, and Dickens. He once wrote of his ten-by-twenty foot room, with its camp-size bed, washstand, and wardrobe: "It is a bit small for an untidy soul, but at least it lessens the size of my untidiness."

It was in the evening when the boys had retired that he found his rest and peace in prayer and in his books.

After the long busy day he would read uninterrupted until his appetite was satiated, until his eyes could see no longer. The silence of the Chinese night in the country, when every sound of human life was hushed, was a pleasure he frequently spoke of. "Be still and see that I am God," said the Psalmist, and Ford, referring to the solitude of his evenings, once said: "In China night comes on as a nurse to lay a coverlet of mist softly and slowly over the sleeping countryside, so that sleep is but a stage of life."

In November 1944, Bishop James Edward Walsh, in his eighth year as Superior General of Maryknoll, managed through the help of the United States Army to get into the Hak-ka mission to make his canonical visitation, and to fly out two of the Maryknollers who were critically ill. Ford, too, was a sick man at the time. Bishop Walsh, reporting back to Maryknoll, wrote of Ford's "calm and unruffled spirit recovering from his bad and painfull illness. He had lost considerable weight," remarked Bishop Walsh; "compared with the last time I saw him eight years ago, he is a skeleton." Bishop Walsh wanted Ford to return with him to the States, but Ford insisted he was improving. Besides he argued, the long dangerous trek through southwest China would be too much for him. Actually, he had no intention of leaving his mission during those troubled days.

All of his missioners had been anxious about his health for some months, but they knew he hated to admit being ill. Throughout his years in China he had succeeded in remaining uncommonly well; his health as far as could be judged had been excellent and for that reason he found it difficult sometimes to understand the indisposition of some of his missioners. He did not show any lack of sympathy in talking to a man who thought he was ill, but he remarked once when a missioner who had come in for a few days rest and recuperation from a bad cold, "You would think the fellow had been visited with the plague."

Now he himself was ill, constantly and wretchedly ill, and there was fear in the mission that he might not recover. Possibly he was aware of this, but he gave no outward sign. His illness did not prevent him from guiding his hostel students, nor from spending hours with any of the United States Navy personnel who cared to visit him, nor from covering his vast mission territory, travelling on foot, by truck, or river boat, always with a notable lack of comfort, conferring Confirmation, meeting his missioners, administrating his vicariate without a chancellor, solving maritial problems without a canon lawyer. His manner remained as calm and his mind remained as keen as ever: he had that facility so often found in great leaders —a dazzling understanding of problems of all sizes, the gift of going straight to the heart of them. How frequently it happens that achievements which surpass the average are the work of men who have below average health. The chronic, painful sprue was the thorn in the flesh; he could not forget it or ignore it, but he would accept it with extraordinary fortitude.

It would be misleading to give the impression that Ford, during those years, was able constantly to maintain his normal buoyancy. At times a certain grayness came over his spirit. He knew he was sick; he was occasionally a bit short tempered, a bit irritable, even with his students. He did his best not to show that grayness to the world, particularly in the presence of the Sisters or his students who always seemed gay and witty in his company. He would wrestle with his depression in prayer and try to lose it in his books during the silent, sleepless hours of the night. But he confided his feelings to no one. Despite his illness during those years, he did maintain his dedication, his generosity. His calm impassive face, his piercing determined dark eyes bespoke his will to continue to the end on the course he set for himself.

Ameliorations, then Yalta

The primary work of the mission, bringing souls to Christ, went on notwithstanding his illness, notwithstanding the interruptions and distractions of the war. Ford was more optimistic than ever before about the future. Some of the causes for the misunderstandings of the past between China and the West were, to a certain extent, being cleared away. For example, on December 9, 1939, Rome had decreed that "it is licit for Catholics to be present at commemorative functions held before a likeness or tablet of Confucius in Confucian shrines or in school," and "inclinations of the head [the kowtow] and other signs of civil respect in the presence of the dead or before their images, or even before a tablet inscribed with the name of the defunct, are also to be regarded as licit and proper." What a pity the Church had to wait until 1939 before Pope Clement XI's ruling on these matters could be reversed.

On January 11, 1943, a different sort of attempt was made to undo the errors of the past. The United States and Britain, in a gesture of good will toward their Chinese allies, abolished extraterritoriality rights and some features of the nineteenth-century "unequal treaties." True, the Western powers at this time had no "rights" in the port cities of China since Japan occupied these areas and had taken over all foreign concessions. Still, the Chinese rejoiced in the political achievement that this document signified. Archbishop Yu Pin remarked, "To the Church, too, it was a boon. Theoretically, her missioners no longer stood under the aegis of the Western powers and their imperialistic aspiration. The missioners should not now be accused of furthering any territorial claims on China."

The establishment of the Chinese hierarchy, putting China on an equal footing in the Church with Christian countries of the West, was another step that pleased the Chinese. The wish to establish the hierarchy according to canonical rule had existed in China for sometime. Early in 1946, the Holy See, recognizing China's emergence as a great world power, issued the papal Bull *Quotidie Nos*, which created the definitive organization of the Church in China. Up to that time the Church was divided into vicariates apostolic and prefectures apostolic; these ecclesiastical divisions were now raised to the status of dioceses. Christians and non-Christians alike welcomed Rome's decision. The Chinese government showed its appreciation by establishing diplomatic relations with the Vatican.

There had been a number of Chinese bishops before —six had been consecrated in Rome in October 1926. Now from among the Chinese clergy, Rome elevated several more priests to the rank of bishop, one to the rank of archbishop, and another to the dignity of cardinal. A large number of newly established dioceses were alloted to Chinese prelates. In 1947, of the 144 dioceses in China, twenty-seven—including Shanghai, Peking, and Canton, the chief centers of Chinese Catholic life—were under Chinese bishops. There were, according to Fides News Service, 2,547 Chinese priests engaged in the ministry and almost six thousand Chinese young men studying for the priesthood. In addition 4,735 native Chinese Sisters were teaching in Catholic schools and instructing converts. The Church in China stood free at last, free—at least theoretically —from the stigma of association with military and political invaders. As Archbishop Yu Pin said at that time: "Our nation is taking its historical step toward constitutional democracy. And for the Church—never before in her history in China, has she faced such golden opportunities. At this critical moment when China needs the Church's help, she stands resplendent with a new life, ready to accompany China along the untrodden ways of her future."

How little did the leaders of the Christian minority in China understand the restlessness of so many Chinese people, the dissatisfaction with and distrust of all things Western, including its religion. How much they, along with the political leaders of the West, underestimated the power and the mission of the Communists. Perhaps toward the conclusion of World War II, the optimism of men like Yu Pin and Ford was understandable. The image of the Church as a small group of "rice Christians" was changing. Archbishop Yu Pin was planning an elite of young Chinese priests from all over China to begin an apostolate to the literati and to the official class in Nanking. Understandably, many bishops were reluctant to deprive their own dioceses of the talents and services of promising young national priests to whom they looked for local leadership. However, a start was made toward the establishment of this special ecclesiastical task force; but there was considerable doubt that it would immediately make the impact expected by the directors of the program.

Bishop Ford in the summer of 1945 quoted a thoughtful Chinese who said that soon there would be many Christian martyrs in China. When the Bishop asked him the reason for this, he explained that with the arrival of Chinese bishops on the scene, the Church would be obliged to take a public stand on political issues which affect moral principles. It was the layman's opinion that the Chinese bishops "ex officio" should lead their people both in patriotism and in rectifying social injustices; there would follow then an alignment of forces for or against the Church on a purely doctrinal basis. This would inevitably lead to some sort of persecution. Ford did not say whether or not the Chinese layman—or he, himself—had in mind the onrush of Communism.

During the years of World War II in China, there were very few public demonstrations of anti-Western sentiment. The United States was regarded with enthusiasm, not only because it was China's ally, but also because it relinquished the humiliating extraterritoriality rights in 1943. At this same time the United States Congress passed the bill that permitted Chinese to migrate to America and, for the first time since 1882 (since the Chinese Exclusion Law), the United States government allowed them to become naturalized American citizens. The Cairo Declaration in November 1943, signed by Roosevelt, Churchill, and Chiang Kai-shek, promising the return of Manchuria, Taiwan, and the Pescadores to China, helped the United States' prestige and Chiang's as well.

The enthusiam, however, was short lived. In February 1945, Roosevelt, Churchill, and Stalin met at Yalta and without consulting with Chiang decided (1) to make Manchuria a Russian sphere of influence; (2) to give Outer Mongolia (over which China claimed jurisdiction) its independence; (3) to internationalize Dairen; (4) to make Port Arthur a Russian naval base. These concessions were granted to Russia in exchange for the Soviet Union's promise to enter the war against Japan (despite MacArthur's insistence that the help of Russia would be unnecessary). Understandably, in China there was strong resentment against the Yalta agreement when Chiang and the Chinese people, months later, learned of the secret accord.

Chiang, of course, was helpless. He could do nothing without United States assistance. He was angry that Stalin's Soviet Union was to receive so many special concessions that Lenin had condemned and renounced in 1919. And events proved that Russian help was superfluous. Only after the first atomic bomb was dropped on Hiroshima on August 6, 1945, did the Soviet army march into Manchuria. They were in a very good position to aid the Chinese Communists when Japan capitulated.

The United States Navy installation moved out of Kaying two weeks after the Japanese surrendered. Some of the Naval officers expressed doubt that the job in the Orient was really finished. One officer remarked just as he was leaving: "We'll be called back within five years." He wasn't far off. In 1951, America was again fighting in the Orient on the cold, barren hills of Korea.

Apparently, few people in Washington understood what had been taking place in China. Few seemed to realize that neither the Nationalists nor the Communists were as concerned with the struggle against Japan as they were with the struggle for ultimate control of their own country. Certainly Bishop Ford did not anticipate any trouble. For him the surrender of Japan meant the end of hostilities. "Now," he wrote, "the opportunities are to be taken advantage of." He was sure the people would recall the mission's efforts to help the refugees and would be more than ever receptive to the gospel message. Politically, China and the West seemed to be friends. The past would be forgotten. The outlook was promising. The Church would now flourish and grow.

"A new China will turn to the United States for help and example." This is what Ford wrote; this is what he believed, although he did not wish to see China American-ized. He foresaw more emphasis by the Chinese on engineering programs, industrial development, and modern agriculture. He knew that the technological tools of the West would be introduced more widely into the Chinese mainstream.

If China was to be transformed into a modern industrial nation, Ford realized that the Church could not ignore this goal. This indicated a change in his thinking with respect to the missioners' responsibility in this area. He saw that the missioner would have to understand at least the sociological problems associated with these changes; though he still would not wish to see the missioner involved full time in the details of economic development. "It might pay us," he said in the spirit of the Church's new role in the social and economic area, "to emphasize somewhat these items of education among our seminarians at Mary-knoll. Much good can be accomplished by priests equipped for handling social and industrial problems and youth services."

In a 1946 letter to Maryknoll, Bishop Ford suggested that the future missioners coming to China be equipped in knowledge of "cooperatives and music, in mass communications and youth work as well as social and economic problems." He proposed what has since been done at Maryknoll—the substitution of "summer courses for our seminarians" in place of the former medical training in hospitals. Ford reported that he received requests for technical aid "in all sorts of projects from starting an ice factory to organizing a band and building a bridge." And he admitted, "These may not be, strictly speaking, priestly works, but they could be opportunities turned to the advantage of the Church."

But the youth of China turned not to the United

States for leadership and direction, but to the Soviet Union —not to Christianity for spiritual and moral guidance, but to atheistic Communism. They wanted no part of that West which had humiliated them for so many years. They were revolutionaries who would throw off the capitalist yoke as the Soviet Union had done.

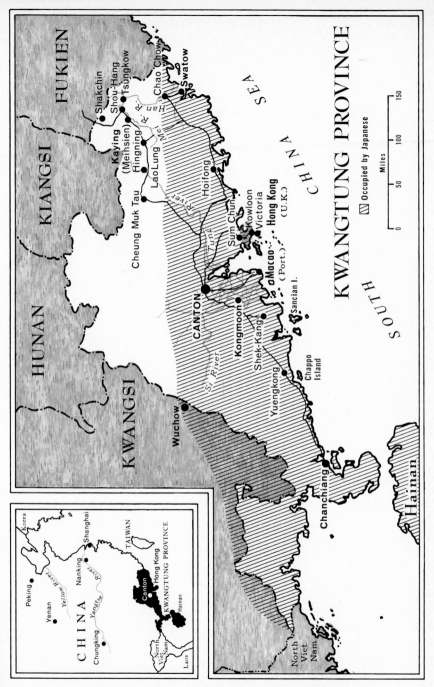

1. *Maryknoll's first mission was in Yuengkong. Bishop Ford's See city was Kaying.*

2. *Francis Ford with his father Austin B. Ford, the publisher of the "Irish World."*

3. *Apple harvest at Maryknoll, autumn 1915. Seminarians Vogel, Meyer, and Ford are in the foreground.*

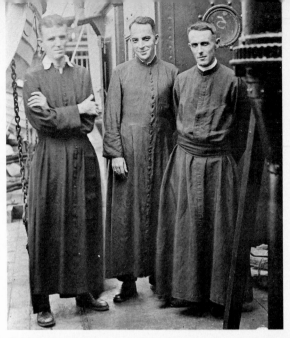

4. Dockside meeting, Hong Kong, 1926. Father Cody Ecstein (r.) is greeted by Ford and James Edward Walsh. Walsh, who was made bishop a year later, has been imprisoned in Shanghai since 1958 on charges of spying.

5. The large building partially hidden by trees housed a Maryknoll mission in the Kongmoon district near Yeunkong.

6. *Inner t'ang of a Chinese farmhouse with a Chris-tian altar. In a pagan household this hall would con-tain ancestral tablets.*

7. *Panoramic view of the city of Kaying (Meishien), made December 1, 1946, shows typical riverboat (r.). Fifty to sixty people with their gear could be fitted into the boat's two layers. The trip from Kaying to Swatow took five days. Sampans (l.) carry freight. They are propelled by manpower or are towed behind the motorized riverboats.*

8. *Road near Fukien border in area where Father Harry Bush was captured by bandits in 1935.*

9. *Kaying Seminary buildings under construction, 1931.*

10. *Monsignor Ford in courtyard of the Wong house, Kaying, 1934.*

11. Ford and the attending bishops at his consecration at Maryknoll, September 21, 1935. Bishop James Anthony Walsh, Superior General and co-founder of Maryknoll, is seated on Bishop Ford's left.

12. Hostel students, Kaying, 1945, with the author, Bishop Ford, and Father Anthony Tsoc.

13. Bishop Francis Xavier Ford
as he appeared one year
after his consecration.

14. First ordination of Chinese priests held at Kaying, June 1949. In
background is roofed-over first floor of the still incompleted cathedral.

 # CHAPTER VII

LAO TZU

*There are those who will conquer the world
And make of it what they conceive or desire.
I see that they will not succeed.
For the world is God's own Vessel.
It cannot be made by human interference.*
          The Wisdom of Lao Tsu, LIN YUTANG, page 164

JESUS CHRIST

*And do not be afraid of those who kill the body
but cannot kill the soul. But rather be afraid of him
who is able to destroy both soul and body in hell.*
                              MATTHEW 10:28

A Native Church

In the summer of 1946, a very sick Bishop Ford was called back to Maryknoll for the General Chapter of the Society which was held every ten years. During the months he spent in the States, he received excellent medical care and his health was restored in an amazing manner. The following summer he left his homeland for the last time, on the way back to his beloved Hak-kas.

Bishop Ford returned to Kaying with renewed vigor and some much-needed cash gathered in America. Immediately he launched upon the final plans for his Center House and cathedral. Several years previously he had purchased a suitable piece of property two hundred yards from the Chinese house that served as the temporary church. The non-Christians were certain that he had consulted a soothsayer before obtaining the land! From their point of view, it was ideally situated, every aspect of the deep-rooted "wind and water" superstition was fulfilled. It was in perfect position on the west bank of the broad Mei River, at the point where the murky brown current makes its "favorable" bend around the city. Bamboo trees, the refined and graceful symbol of longevity and modesty, lined the edge of the property, where river boats and sampans took refuge from the sun in the cool, dark shadows along the bank of the sluggish stream. The wind and water approached the propitious plot from a satisfactory angle bringing blessings on those who dwelt thereon. There was enough Irish in Ford not to argue with this essential belief; he understood the superstition and jokingly hinted that the ancient cult was a factor in his choice of the property.

He had, however, more pragmatic reasons for selecting the site: "approach to the market, proximity to the main highway, possibility of radiating in all directions, suitability of terrain, ease in buying it and, lastly, opportunity for future growth."

On the new site, the convent for the Sisters and the parish house for the priests assigned to the cathedral had already been constructed. The next building was to be the Mission Center House, a combination chancery, bishop's residence, and student's hostel. Ford had been living all his priestly life in rented Chinese houses, and for almost seven years he had occupied the same house with some thirty middle school boys. He was now ready to get into a house of his own. Also he was finding it more and more taxing to entertain missioners coming to Kaying for vacation, though he did admit that the men needed a society house where they could relax. "Bishops" he said, "are supposed to exercise hospitality, but I'm a poor host by nature." During the war, travel was difficult and visitors to Kaying were few, but as conditions improved, more and more priests were arriving at the Center to make purchases in Kaying, or to obtain medical attention, or rest, and he felt compelled to rush construction on his new Center House.

The building was necessarily a large one. Ford wrote: "The roominess of the place has helped me to keep calm . . . the electric light and the showers give the priests the illusion of a vacation when they stop in."

Ford was acutely sensitive to the fact that people would point to it as the residence of the Catholic bishop. To counteract criticism of its size, he invited the hostel students to share the house, even if it meant some noisy inconvenience for himself and the visiting priests. A few missioners did not take kindly to the idea of thirty-five middle school students living in the Center House. After living for several months in a remote mission station, they felt they should have a quiet place for reading and relaxation. However, Ford did not intend to have a spacious half-empty house as an episcopal mansion. In Kaying the bishop would live in a student's hostel.

While the Center House was going up, Ford was busy with his good friend the Chinese architect K. S. Kit, drawing up plans for his cathedral. When he had first rented a shop in Kaying city and converted it into a makeshift chapel, Ford had promised his small congregation that one day they would have a real church, "as soon as you can pay for it yourselves." The Christian community had grown, and even the large rented quarters in the Wong house had become inadequate. Ford conceded that "our determination to build only when the Christians had contributed sufficient funds for the new church gradually weakened." But the conviction that the cathedral should be the expression of their faith sustained him, and their sacrifices justified his hopes. His dream of the cathedral included a "local padre," a priest of the soil, as its pastor.

A conversation with the Apostolic Delegate, Archbishop Riberi, suggested to him the appropriateness of erecting a church that expressed Chinese artistic taste. In Chinese architecture there are embodied various geomantic, religious, and artistic ideas that are at the very root of Chinese civilization. Ford tried to translate some of these ideas into adobe. "Chinese art," the Delegate remarked, "has served Buddhism and Confucianism for centuries, we must now baptize it." Bishop Ford needed little urging, since he was of the same mind. Past errors in this regard were irreparable; future errors would be inexcusable. He personally preferred Chinese architecture to Western designs, and he insisted on this with Mr. Kit. But to achieve a practical building of Chinese style adequate for the liturgy demanded much thought. He had no intention of making a slavish imitation of the Chinese temple; he would make an adaptation of its best features.

"Chinese temples," he said, "if enlarged, would present a forest of columns to obstruct the worshiper's view. Moreover, though the dark interiors are awesome in effect, they bespeak more the nether regions and are alien to the joyous Easter message." Since the entire congregation in a Chinese parish followed the Mass, and chanted in unison the appropriate prayers (long before the recent liturgical reform),

Ford insisted that the church should allow a well-lighted, unobstructed view of the altar and permit the people to gather around it with the priest. "The one advantage of the temple style," he wrote, "which can be adapted easily, is the placing of the altar in the center of the building, not at one end. This will make the long axis the facade, with pleasing symmetry."

When his cathedral was completed, he wanted it to be visible from as many angles and to as many people as possible: "The long stretch of the river on either side prolongs the vista, and boatmen a mile away will be able to glimpse the cathedral before they see the city."

"The building will soon rise," he wrote enthusiastically to Maryknoll as construction got under way. No time was lost. During the architectural planning, sand, lime, and clay for the cathedral were being piled high on the riverside property, each basketful weighed and paid for on the spot. Hundreds of women, with the rhythmic sway of dancers, were wearing a path to the construction site, emptying their baskets, trudging off for more.

Ford was proud that the materials would be local, would be carried by local Christians for the most part, and would be paid for by their sacrifices. Its walls, he wrote, were to be "pounded and kneaded into shape out of the very material nature supplies us with close at hand." The altar would be of local granite, the pews made from nearby trees floated down the river, the roof tiles baked by Christians less than a mile away.

Ford yielded to a personal indulgence by building alongside his cathedral a seven-tiered pagoda. Pagodas are an essential element of the Chinese landscape. Originally in China the ever present towers contained holy relics of Buddha. The pagoda was an integral part of Buddhist faith and worship. There was a widely prevailing taboo among the people that calamities would befall those who used a pagoda for purposes other than religious, but the taboo did not bother Ford. He had in mind several non-religious purposes for his pagoda.

Still, he was concerned about the innovation. "Are we justified," he asked, "in indulging in such a non-essential structure?" He admitted that strickly speaking, he probably was not. In a letter to Maryknoll, Ford explained the usages to which he would put his pagoda: "Pagodas, like the round towers of Ireland, are usually picturesque but useless, except as landmarks for footsore travellers, telling them they are near their destination. Chinese architectural principles do not permit us to put a steeple on the church. The pagoda will solve the need for a landmark, the graceful tower will become the prize subject of hundreds of Chinese Kodak fans." And it would be crowned with a cross. He wanted to lift the Church out of the catacombs of rented shops and farmhouses: "The cross atop the pagoda will dominate the entire city," the Church would no longer be "hidden away in low buildings." Furthermore, to introduce some modern conveniences, he would use one story of the pagoda as a water storage tank; in another story he planned to install a generator. The highest level would contain the cathedral bell.

As soon as the first level of the cathedral could be roofed, Ford decided to put the structure into service. The historic move from the Wong house to the new property and its still unfinished cathedral was made on a Sunday in December 1948, when a large percentage of the Christians were present. Ford was amused by what he referred to as the "liturgical flourish" that accompanied the efficient transportation of the chapel furnishings. The pastor, dressed in cope and surplice, solemnly led the triumphant procession; the congregation followed carrying church benches, candlesticks, altar furnishings, vestments, Stations of the Cross, carpets, and everything that was movable. The Catholic Church in Kaying had at last its own property, its own church, and its own living quarters for bishop, priests, and Sisters. But the bright future that was anticipated on that happy occasion was soon to be darkened by the portentous clouds of the approaching cataclysm.

The Seeds Take Root

In 1943, Chiang Kai-shek published two books, *China's Destiny* and *Chinese Economic Ideology*. He blamed imperialism and the unequal treaties for China's plight and pledged the implementation of Sun Yat-sen's three principles of the people—Nationalism, Democracy, and People's Livelihood. For Chiang this was to be the final fulfillment of China's goals, economic as well as political. Mao Tse-tung, leader of the Communists, also regarded the implementation of these three principles as appropriate—but only during what he called the transitional period. The ideological differences between the Nationalists and the Communists, whatever the goals, was ultimately to be decided in a contest of physical strength.

With the surrender of the Japanese in August 1945, the Chinese Nationalists and Communists competed for control of Japanese-held areas of China. It was estimated at the time that the Nationalists possessed a five-to-one superiority in combat troops and munitions. The United States transported three of Generalissimo Chiang's armies north to take the surrender of about one million Japanese and their equipment. But the Communist guerillas, located in the north and central areas, held a geographical advantage, and in the more remote regions the Communists forced some Japanese units to surrender to them. It was in Manchuria where the Russians were in occupation that the Chinese Communists, aided by the Soviets, seized large supplies of Japanese arms and military equipment in direct violations of the 1945 Sino-Soviet treaty and the Yalta agreement, which specified that no Chinese group other than the Nationalists should be assisted.

Several months later when the government troops tried to enter Manchuria they were opposed by the Chinese Communists, already well organized and equipped. Early in 1946 the Nationalists threw their best armies into the Manchurian campaign and succeeded in establishing a tenuous control. Their operations, however, depended on a supply line one thousand miles long: they had committed themselves to a project they could not support. This overextension opened the way to the eventual piecemeal destruction of the Nationlist units by the Communists, whose military policy was never to commit their major forces in combat. A rift between the Kuomintang officials and the Nationalist military command in Manchuria contributed to the disintegration and seriously lowered the morale of government troops. Conversely, as the Communists bled the strength of the Nationalists and destroyed their lines of communication, their morale mounted and many well-equipped Nationalist troops defected to the Communist ranks.

It seemed evident as 1946 drew to a close that the government, while appreciating the danger, had underestimated not only the Communist military strength and its tactical skill, but the popular sentiment as well. The Nationalists throughout the north and west had extended themselves and stretched their lines of communications. They had neither sufficient troops to garrison the key positions, nor the personnel to administer them. Unlike the Communist guerillas, who lived off the land, the government troops had to be supplied from bases in central China. Futhermore, the Nationalists failed to present programs that would improve the social and economic life of the people; they failed also to provide efficient local administrations.

Politically there was in China a lack of a democratic tradition. The Nationalist regime had, since 1927, been operating under the theory of political tutelage. Had the Kuomintang remained the dynamic, revolutionary force conceived of by Sun Yat-sen, it might have been effective. But no political organization is better than its leaders, and the leaders, being human, are subject to human frailties. There was no opposition party to serve as watchdog, no popular elections to threaten the position of the officials. Party leaders were the power elite and most of them gradually lost touch with the masses. There were Chinese Nationalist government officials of outstanding loyalty and personal integrity. Yet many of Chiang's officials had accumulated great wealth and large land holdings. Not all these men were "bad": they were perhaps no different, no more corrupt than officials who preceded them in other regimes or other dynasties in China. But officialdom had become the country's "most lucrative industry." The leaders were for years on end the same men, no new leaders were being trained; loyalty to the party leadership was the criterion for membership and advancement. The men in power insisted on the *status quo* and they frustrated the ambitions of younger men who looked for a dynamic formula that would save their country from decay.

There is no evidence that Chiang himself was corrupt. Whatever shortcomings he had, he appeared honest and certainly he was not a quitter. Possibly he had not understood all the needs of his people. Repeatedly during World War II, he reminded the people: "China has two diseases, one of the heart and one of the skin. The disease of the skin (Japan) will soon be checked. The disease of the heart (Communism) is far more serious." Nevertheless, the Nationalist government seemed unwilling or unable to think in social and economic terms in its approach to the people and in its crusade against Communism. To regard Communism as a purely military issue was a mistake. Communism would have collapsed long ago had it not represented a crusade against injustices, real or fabricated.

It is questionable if any political leader could have accomplished more in a country so torn with internal strife from the moment he took office. Chiang came to power shortly before China was attacked by powerful Japan in Manchuria in 1932. That fight continued with a break of only a few years, to the end of World War II. Despite the unsettled conditions, those who were in China during the thirties and forties did see many evidences of progress, many new schools, new roads, and some new industry. What has happened on Taiwan during the past ten years is an evidence of what the Nationalists could do—with American help, it is true—to improve the economy and stabilize the government. But on the mainland it was not enough.

In August 1945 United States Ambassador Patrick J. Hurley brought Mao Tse-tung and Chiang together in Chungking, but nothing came of the meeting. In November President Truman sent General George Marshall to mediate between the two antagonists. Marshall, however, was placed in an untenable position. While he was mediating on the one hand between two Chinese groups, the United States government continued to supply arms to the Nationalist side. After a year of fruitless effort to effect a compromise, Marshall resigned and returned to Washington. He had little hope that the major issues between the two factions could be settled by democratic procedures. There was too much deep-seated distrust on both sides.

Meanwhile United States Ambassador John Leighton Stuart, who succeeded Hurley, was sending reports to Washington indicating a "steady deterioration of morale in the Government forces." He also reported the students' strike in June and July of 1947. In every major academic center in China students, with much sympathy from university faculties, demanded an end to the civil war and effective government action to improve the national economic situation. The demonstrations had strong anti-American overtones. Only the early closing of the universities prevented more serious disturbances. The mounting discontent was apparent and the Communist prestige was, as a consequence, gaining. Many United States advisors in China seemed to see in the Communists the liberators of the people's permanent oppression, the destroyers of corruption in government, the builders of a peaceful, prosperous nation.

In July, 1947 President Truman sent General Albert C. Wedemeyer on a fact-finding mission to China. Wedemeyer's report was not encouraging. "I find apathy and lethargy in many quarters," he wrote. His suggestion to remove incompetent and corrupt leaders was applauded by the Liberal opposition within the Kuomintang. But in most Nationalist quarters his report was rejected on the grounds that he had not sought his information impartially. The United States government felt that no amount of aid could now alter the situation.

In early 1947 Mao had warned his followers that they should prepare for a long hard struggle of at least five years. He did not anticipate the speedy disintegration of Chiang's army nor the amazing victories his forces were to achieve in their sweeping southward march. By the end of 1949, all of China proper had been brought under Communist control.

On October 1, 1949, at the famous T'ien-an-men Square in Peking, Mao established the People's Republic of China. In his speech that day Mao said China was determined to catch up, overtake, and then go on the offensive and make the West suffer for the past. He said precisely what he knew the people wanted to hear: "We will work bravely and diligently to create our own civilization and happiness, and will, at the same time, promote world peace and freedom. Our country will never again be an insulted nation. . . ." China would no longer be a passive, helpless nation.

In another speech at about the same time, Mao proclaimed: "Once man has eliminated capitalism he will attain the era of perpetual peace, and there will be no more need for war." He expressed his conviction that this utopia would be achieved only by force of arms. The Chinese Communist leaders believe that struggle—and they specify "violent, mortal struggle"—is inevitable as long as class society exists.

China's youth wanted to take the offensive against the West—not only to hit out, but to hit back. They wanted to feel that they could hold their own against the West. Four centuries of impotence, subjection, and humiliation seemed far too long a time. Any length of time, however short or long, is bound to seem interminable to anybody who has to pass it as underdog.

Four vital factors favored Mao and tipped the balance of power in favor of the Communists. (1) He was more aggressively anti-West than the Nationalists; the student population and the young intellectuals felt that Chiang was committed to the West and that he could not survive if he let go the apron strings of the United States. (2) Mao was able to convince the peasants that he could do more for them in righting social injustices and in bettering their economic welfare. (3) The Communist officials appeared to live like the common people. They enjoyed no luxuries or excesses. (4) Mao promised to reduce taxes, to liquidate the landlords, and to redivide the land, even though he probably knew that scarcity of land was as great a problem as redistribution. This program roused the peasants to arms —the final victory for the Communist forces.

In the fall of 1947, after his return from furlough in America, Ford for the first time felt apprehensive. In a letter to Maryknoll he wrote: "I doubt if 'southern' Communism for many years will be able to rouse antagonism against the Church, as the war gave the Church much opportunity of proving its interest in the welfare of the common people. The war seems to have taken the attention of the masses away from the Church as a foreign institution. I do not think this is subjective wishing on my part. We shall continue our catechumenates and improve the liturgical life of our parishes. I confidently predict, now that we have peace, we shall resume our successful work with less effort and with perhaps greater results." But then he added, "Much will depend, of course, on the progress of the Communists and the form it takes in this region."

It was Ford's opinion—and many agreed with him at the time—that the Communists, to succeed wholly, would have to destroy what China had always valued most: the family and community loyalties. With what would they replace the traditional Chinese family? How could a system of power and order be established outside of and apart from the family? These reasonable questions seemed difficult to answer. Within human history tyrants have been able to force an unwilling people to submit for a limited time to arbitrary dictates and innovations that had no roots in the society upon which they were imposed, but they had never been able successfully to force upon their subjects a pattern of life that was contrary to their wishes.

Ford observed the Chinese Communists' police-state tactics, their hard, high-powered propaganda, rigidly controlled schools, youth movements, and demonstrations—tools to shape a new generation of Chinese into the desired form—and he doubted that they would ever succeed. "It will require several generations," he said, "years of unflagging effort, and an ever expanding number of dedicated adherents who will be willing to give their lives to the cause."

Well-acquainted with Chinese history, Ford knew that it was not a new thing for the Chinese to revolt against the ruling power. But in the past, it was never a revolt against a way of life, never an attempt to reform or change existing customs. The historic Chinese revolution was an attempt on the part of the people to rid themselves of an unjust ruler, not to destroy established traditions, however evil. Until the advent of Communism, the people did not wish to change the structural arrangement of Chinese society. Civil strife was always a contest between men, not ideologies. Furthermore, the peasants had never before attempted to seize for themselves the reins of government. Once the evil ruler was removed, they would return to their way of life, quite willing to obey the newcomers who would carry on in traditional fashion.

In 1949 Ford, commenting on the change that was taking place, saw the change merely as a "veil over the older civilization." He judged the old system to be "permanent, and the modern [Communist system] a veneer."

Ford highly respected the Confucianist way of life that had so basically influenced the Chinese throughout the centuries; he felt it was in many ways close to Christianity. Confucianism taught that a good society was one in which each individual occupied his proper place. "When the individual is right, the family is right; when the family is right, the nation is right; and when the nation is right, all under heaven will be right." It was the Confucian emphasis on fulfilling the duties inherent in the five human relationships that particularly appealed to Ford: between emperor and subject, father and son, husband and wife, between brothers, and between friends. And he felt certain Communism would never supplant this Confucian tradition.

During the period of the civil war's heavy fighting in China's far north, Kaying was relatively quiet. The Koumintang officials remained at the county seat and the armed garrison seemed relaxed and confident. Occasionally middle school students staged anti-American demonstrations and rallies for the cessation of hostilities. In nearby villages Communist guerillas from time to time attacked the homes of wealthy landowners to obtain food. However, as reports of Communist victories in the north reached the Kaying area, the local guerilla forces grew and their activities increased. Even before the main Communist army crossed the Yangtze on April 20, 1949, the city of Kaying was captured by

Kwangtung's Communist guerillas without a shot being fired. The garrison and most of the Kuomintang officials had fled; those who remained were put to death. Prisons were emptied of Communist sympathizers and refilled with those who were known to oppose the new regime.

Chiang Kai-shek and the Nationalist government, realizing that the Communists could not be checked, abandoned the mainland and with about 400,000 troops retreated to the offshore island of Taiwan.

Ford and the rest of the missioners feared that the mission work would be, for a time, at least, interrupted. None of them realized fully the ultimate peril that was in store. After all, a change was needed, errors and injustices had to be righted; perhaps the new regime would, in fact, establish an order of equity and peace. Mission efforts would then be able to continue in a land free of wars and free from injustices.

The Catholic bishops in China had already determined in October 1948 that all foreign missioners were to remain at their posts until forcibly expelled. At a meeting of his own priests, early in 1949, Ford, for the first time publicly voiced his concern for the safety of the mission. He said, "In the present circumstances, the persecution is not purely nor mainly antiforeign, but also antireligious. Hence, flight would be a negative apostasy or at least a dereliction of duty, a failure to minister to our people at the very moment they especially need spiritual aid to witness for Christ. This ministry, of course, demands prudence. . . ."

Still hopeful that some form of coexistence was possible, he added, "It is moreover deemed a fact that the persecution is not imminent, at least for a year or more. The Reds have shown themselves less menacing as they become stronger; they have publicly promised protection to religious institutions and services. Missioners who prematurely fled their regions, on returning have been treated with liberty and even material support by the Red authorities." He concluded, "We cannot abandon our flock in this spiritual crisis, we are obliged by our priestly office and by love to identify ourselves with our people."

By May of 1949, it was evident the Communists would soon be in control of the entire area. Ford was becoming uneasy. For inter-mission communications the missioners had been using World War I Knights of Columbus stationery, on the letterheads of which was the American flag. Shortly after Ford reached Kaying the mission received a large shipment of the surplus supply from the States. Early in 1948 the Bishop had cautioned the missioners about using the letterheads, and he was greatly annoyed to receive at this time a note from a Maryknoller written on the stationery. "Common prudence," he impatiently announced, "would suggest that such letterheads are open to dangerous ambiguity. Hence, I repeat, priests and Sisters are forbidden their use, and should not keep them without immediately removing the identification of their origin. Possession of such letterheads in these jittery days is dangerous. Thoughtless users continue to expose us all to suspicion."

He continued to keep his missioners informed, sending out bits of news as he received them. He told of the investigation of an outlying mission: "The Reds, after taking an inventory of the rectory, said the missioner had too many towels and too many beds, adding that the rectory was too big and should be torn down." While inspecting this rectory, every piece of correspondence was carefully examined by men fluent in English. Letters and memoranda that might even remotely be regarded as incriminating, were confiscated. Most missioners did burn all material pertaining to Communism or to the Nationalist regime and any letter from a United States military person. But some, including the Bishop himself, were careless in this regard.

In June, Ford wrote to Maryknoll: "We should thank God that the turnover two weeks ago was effected without violence and without much excitement. Here at the Center, proclamations were made that religion was to be protected, and, de facto, few, even of the idle newly-enrolled Liberators, have wandered through our property and none has entered our buildings. The attendance at Mass on Sunday has been normal and Catholics have come in even from some of the villages. The Communist Social Affairs inspector visited us and assured us that we both were working for the same ends—we by spiritual means, they with material aims. . . . He also told us we were free to circulate as usual without restrictions."

Despite the unsettled conditions and the pervasive fear that gripped everyone, on Christmas 1949 a record number of the faithful came to Mass. Apparently their religious devotion had increased with the Communist oppression. The Christians seemed to sense that the new government might take away their cathedral, as had been done in the north, and deprive them of the comforts of their religion. These thoughts made their faith suddenly more precious than ever before. Strangely, a number of non-Christians came to the church for instruction in the Christian doctrine during this first year, even though this was frowned upon by the Communist authorities.

Jubilantly, Ford wrote at this time, "Perhaps the most glorious page in Chinese history is now being written by the devotion of both Chinese priests and Chinese Christians. There has been little panic and there is a surprising demonstration of fidelity to the faith. Almost overnight the Christian community has been recognized, even by many puzzled non-Christians, as the one religious force in evidence throughout China, not necessarily an endorsement of the Nationalist regime, but clearly taking a stand on moral and doctrinal issues"—such as parental authority and the permanence of the family, the right to own property and the right of assembly.

His initial contact with the Communist authorities convinced Ford that he was correct about the Chinese brand of communism. He explained his position in a circular letter to his priests: "It might be well to recall that Communism in the Balkan States is conditioned quite differently from China. In the Balkans, where the majority are Christians, the Communists are concentrating on Catholicism and they are propagating atheism, and the Church, through the ballot, has a chance of arousing opposition in a relatively enlightened congregation. In China, Communism is more political than anti-religious and is striving for military supremacy rather than radical social change . . . the persecution of the Church is mostly local . . . the vast majority of the people should not be called Communists in the strict sense of conviction . . . Chinese Communism *ex professo* has promised freedom of worship and protection of Church property." Ford really wanted to believe this; he tried to ignore the experience the Kaying mission had with the Reds in 1928.

Gradually, however, the truth became evident, and reluctantly Ford reported the sad facts: "Restrictions," he wrote early in 1950, "are much more frequent, but they are merely tantalizing, interminable delays in getting permission to travel, with photos galore each time."

In the spring of 1950, Bishop James E. Walsh in Shanghai was placed under house arrest. (Walsh had refused to co-operate in the establishment of the Chinese Catholic Church which was to be separated from Rome. He was also found guilty of speaking against the People's Democratic Republic, and because he refused voluntarily to leave the country, he was confined to his residence. In 1958 he was convicted of espionage on behalf of the United States government and sentenced to twenty years imprisonment.) Ford himself was restricted to the city limits of Kaying. At this time he commented briefly in a letter to Maryknoll on the health and spirits of the Sisters and his priests, thanking God that they remained good. Then he added: "The next year will be the real test, the Lord can see us through if He wishes." He had a conviction of the "permanency of the Church in China," that he did not have before. A large number of people seemed to be in sympathy with the Church and the old order it represented.

During the first year of the occupation, there were executions of landowners who protested and of villagers found with weapons in their homes: a few who were known to have spoken out against Communism simply disappeared. Otherwise, during the first year the Reds were friendly and affable. They were full of zeal for the new cause in which they obviously believed. Enthusiastic, dedicated young people predominated. They were sure that China, with Russia's help, would rid the country of western imperialism and eventually conquer the West. These youngsters were sure they would have a place in the new industrialized China. Ironically, the tools and techniques they would use would all be from the West they hated.

Soon, however, the attempt at concord gave way to tension and strife. More and more businesses were taken over by the new government or taxed out of existence.

Suicides became common, despair set in. Violence was the new weapon, fear was the result. Food became scarce, work was impossible to find. "Kill—Hate" rallies were held daily against the old regime and against the foreigners. Shopkeepers and independent landowners, or anyone unsympathetic with Communism, saw now that there was no way to resist; prudence dictated submission. Those who resisted change were at first cautioned, then threatened. If they still refused to fall in line, they were imprisoned, and not a few were put to death. Among the poor, there was no reason to resist. They had nothing with which to resist. They had no understanding of the Communist philosophy. They thought only of peace and the chance of a better life. Most of the youth had broken with the past or had fled. Those who remained felt they had little to lose by going along with the new order.

By this time, in the outlying districts, all public worship was disallowed. Most of the Chinese priests were directed to return to their homes. Some of the churches were confiscated and used by the liberators for indoctrination centers or for granaries. The Communists insisted that there was still "freedom of religion," but according to the new regulations there was to be no "freedom of assembly." Thus the churches had to be closed down.

Finally realizing the futility of trying to carry on the mission's work, Ford ordered the native Sisters to discard their religious habits, disband, and return to their homes until conditions improved.

Through 1950, Ford was still able to communicate with his missioners. True, he was not permitted to leave the city, but the prohibition was merely for "his protection." His last monthly letter written at Pentecost exhorted his priests and Sisters to be ready to suffer, just as Christ their leader suffered. He did not want them to rebel against suffering and thereby poison themselves spiritually. "Pain and suffering," he said, "may be God's plan to purify our motives. Pain accepted in advance may be God's way to unite us more closely to Himself. 'If they have hated me, they will hate you also.' You must not expect heaven on earth. As Christians we must share the cross. Perhaps suffering is the only way we can expiate the sins of the world, our own and others. This should not worry or terrify us. 'I can do all things in Him who gives me strength.'"

Insofar as he could get the information, Ford had studied the Communist tactics in other territories. Now he saw them at work in his own diocese: the antireligious propaganda, the suppression of all public expression of religion, the rigid control of all news and information, and the prohibition against all public gatherings and criticism. Those with surplus food had to yield it. Many were still hungry, all who would resist were helpless. They were far from the utopia they had been promised. The destiny of the people was in the hands of a small group of officials who maintained their control by promises backed by armed force and terror.

The Communist officials in Kaying evidently followed a time schedule passed down to them from Peking. There was to be no violence for the first few months. This period was to be used to gain the confidence and good will of the people. Evidence was to be gathered to prove that the wealthy landowners had been exploiting the poor. Data on all foreigners was to be collected to show that they were working for the imperialist Western nations that had humiliated China through the years. The program seemed to work satisfactorily: The wealthy were slowly liquidated.

The Maryknoll priests and Sisters were one by one placed under house arrest or taken off to prison. The churches were closed.

Maryknoll Sister Paulita described the last Mass in the market town of Hingning.

> Late in November we had our final Sunday Mass. Father Aloysius Au, our Chinese pastor, had already received notice that for an indefinite time there were to be no further gatherings of the people in church; but he did not accept this notice as official. To avoid trouble, he told the Christians that Sunday Mass would be earlier than the usual hour. Just as the assistant priest, Father John Wong, was nearing the end of the ceremony, a Communist soldier threateningly walked in the side door of the church, hand on gun. He eyed the congregation cautiously and advanced directly to the altar rail. He commanded Father Wong to discontinue the Mass. Father Au, with characteristic courage, approached the soldier and quietly invited him outside for a few words. Father Wong was thus able quickly to complete the ceremony as the frightened Christians chanted the Mass prayers with him. Father Wong signaled to the people to make no more sound and their voices dropped off gradually to whispers. As the priest left the sanctuary the Christians silently and sadly slipped away. It was the last Mass they were to hear, for their pastor was taken prisoner and placed in a labor squad. The church was closed. The Sisters were placed under house arrest.

Sister Paulita recalled that while confined to the convent their guards permitted the Sisters to take a brief walk in the early evening on the basketball court in the rear of the church. Frequently, she said, they would see Father

Au, dirty and weary after his long day of manual labor, come along the road near the church with a group of prisoners. "Clad only in shorts," she said, "his back blackened by the sun, he walked as though in much pain. He was not accustomed to walking on the rough gravel paths without shoes." Father Au, bearing so bravely the inevitable yoke his priesthood had placed on him, would secretly send a scribbled note to the Sisters; he likened his confinement and labor to the life of our Lord. He said he would give the Sisters a blessing as he passed by, and general absolution on Sundays. "Our penance," Sister said, "was to be one decade of the rosary for our persecutors." In another note Au resignedly said: "A few years of suffering in this earthly prison, if God wills it, is not very much." He warned the Sisters not to contact him. "Have courage and confidence in the Lord," he added.

On December 3, 1950, Father Joseph Van den Bogaard and two Maryknoll Sisters were arrested at their Lao Lung mission and led off to the county jail. (They were later deported, as were the other Maryknollers in the region.)

Meanwhile, in Kaying the noose was being pulled tighter and tighter around the Christian community. On December 22, 1950, the entire foreign mission personnel of the cathedral was summoned to police headquarters. Two judges from north China questioned them about the presence of guns and wireless sets at the mission. When they denied any knowledge of such things, they were allowed to return to the mission.

⬡ CHAPTER VIII

MENCIUS

If there should be found the Head of State who does not love to send men to their deaths, the people of the world would lift up their heads, aspiring to enjoy his rule. They would run to him as water which of its own accord flows towards the valleys. Who could withstand such a torrent?

MENCIUS, BOOK I, PART I, CHAPT. VI

JESUS CHRIST

A new commandment I give you, that you love one another: that as I have loved you, you also love one another. By this will all men know that you are my disciples, if you have love for one another.

JOHN 13:34-35

House Arrest

The reality of Communist China was brought home to Ford on the morning of December 23, 1950. Soldiers of the People's Army arrived in two jeeps to seize the Catholic mission. The Sisters and priests of the cathedral staff were taken by surprise and placed under house arrest. Ford protested. He pointed out to the soldiers that the new government expressly promised freedom of religion. But he soon saw the futility of resisting. The soldiers confined him temporarily in his Center House dining room, where he slept on the table. The house was feverishly ransacked. Later in the day three officers came to search the Bishop's files and archives for documents of value to the Communists. During the search, Maryknoll Sister Joan Marie, the Bishop's secretary, was forced to sit in the Bishop's office guarded by two soldiers. "It seemed so melodramatic, so crazy," she said —like a child's treasure hunt that seemed never to end.

Unfortunately, among the papers still intact was the file on Father Harry Bush's capture by brigands in 1935. There were many communications on file about his recapture and release that had been exchanged by Ford and the American consulates in Canton and Swatow and with the United States Embassy in Nanking. They were innocent enough from one point of view, but they were highly incriminating when judged by the Communists, who already believed that Ford was in the employ of the American government. A letterhead bearing the mark of the United States Army Air Force was also discovered in a box in the attic. Additional papers were found, conferences to his missioners, copies of letters sent to America in which Ford condemned Communism and its materialistic and atheistic doctrine. Some of these went back to 1928, when the Reds first struck the Hak-ka hills. With the "evidence" they discovered, the Chinese inspectors accused him of anticommunist, counterrevolutionary, and espionage activities. Ford was placed in solitary confinement in a second-floor bedroom. His Center House–Student Hostel now became his prison. Three other Maryknollers, Fathers James McCormick, Francis White, and James O'Donnell were locked in another room of the house.

While the Maryknollers were being questioned, the Chinese priest Father Lam and some young men had been busy putting the finishing touches on the Christmas decorations and the Crib in the cathedral.

One of the Kaying Christians now living in Hong Kong tells about that Christmas. "In the forenoon of Christmas Eve," he said, "my mother and all the members of our family, old and young, along with about twenty other Christians in our village, all dressed in our best clothes, carrying some food for the journey, started in a joyous mood the ten mile walk to Kaying to attend the joyous feast of Christmas. We talked and laughed as we walked along, joyful and gay. Upon reaching the door of the church, to our consternation, we saw that it was guarded by two Communist soldiers who barred our entrance. On the front door of the church we read a government proclamation issued by the Kaying Public Safety Bureau, stating that no one was to be allowed to enter the church. One of the soldiers told us to return to our homes. 'There will be no ceremony here tonight or tomorrow morning and no one is allowed to see the Bishop or priests—this is an order of the People's government.'

"It was then about one o'clock in the afternoon. We saw many more Christians coming toward the church from distant villages to celebrate the birth of Jesus. In like manner they too paused at the front door of their beloved cathedral and read with dismay that they were not allowed to enter. Under these circumstances there was nothing we could do but sadly return to our homes, which we did with heavy hearts and anxious minds. We had come with joy and happy expectation in our hearts, but we left sorrowfully depressed, not daring to give vent to our indignation and our disappointment."

Meanwhile in the city of Kaying, anti-American demonstrations were intensified. Organized bands of youths with placards displaying Communist slogans and anti-West insults marched across the bridge to demonstrate outside the mission property.

During his house arrest many people from a distance saw Bishop Ford at his second-story window—his people. Some seemed to hide their faces as though they were ashamed of what was taking place. Others, looking closer, noticed that he was becoming gaunt and haggard. In a week he grew old.

Tormented as he was, the Bishop was more anxious about the Sisters, his priests, and his Christians than he was about himself. What would happen to them? Could they stand the strain of questioning? Would his Christians remain loyal to the Church? And what of his cathedral and his Christian pagoda? He had dreamed of the cathedral from the first week in the rented Kaying shop that served as his chapel and his home. The Christians had made sacrifices for it, his friends at home had sent gifts for it. And the pagoda was his pride and joy. "We claim it is the only useful pagoda in China," he had boasted. "Its cross is the highest point in the whole city."

During confinement, Ford was subjected to constant harassment and daily questioning. What was the source of his money? Who paid him and his agents? Who sent him to China? What did he think of the new Chinese government? What part did he have in directing the activities of the American military units stationed in Kaying during the war? Why did the United States naval personnel visit him so frequently? On and on went the interrogation. Papers from his files were brought to him for explanation. His interrogaters insisted that the telegrams to the United States consuls were secret code messages revealing valuable information about China.

Ford could see that his captors were building up a

prejudged case against him. His answers and explanations were scoffed at and rejected. They repeatedly stated that the evidence against him was overwhelmingly conclusive. He had been spying for the United States government; he had been harboring Nationalist agents in his house; anti-Communist organizers were found at the mission hidden in his house; he was in the process of recruiting and leading a "black army" against the People's Government which he slandered in letters and in speeches; he was planning to sabotage the Communist government's attempt to establish a Chinese National Catholic Church.

Pravda reported these charges against Ford and concluded that he was "an important United States agent" in China. All Chinese newspapers carried accounts of his disclosed espionage activities. In Canton a caricature was widely circulated. It showed Bishop Ford pretending to read his prayer book while he treacherously kept watch as Sister Joan Marie signaled on a wireless set to United States planes flying menacingly overhead.

Guilty!

On the morning of April 15, 1951, after almost four months of confinement in his room, without books, without writing paper or pencil, without his pipe or tobacco, with only his rosary and his prayers to comfort him, he and his secretary, Sister Joan Marie, were taken to the municipal building to be tried for espionage. The Bishop and the Sister were bound with rope fastened across their upper arms and chest as a sort of halter from which hung two guide lines held by the soldiers. As he was led away through the courtyard, Ford turned his eyes toward the window where the three confined priests were sadly watching. They were never to see him again.

Thirty soldiers, armed with bayoneted rifles, escorted the Bishop and the Sister across the bridge, along the main street, through a curious, sometimes hostile crowd, to the court room of the county administration building.

The trial was farcical. The evidence of the files was produced. The accusations were leveled against the Bishop and Sister—they were promptly found guilty and sentenced to the provincial prison in Canton as spies against the People's Government. At no point could they plead their innocence. Ford knew that he had already been condemned before the verdict was announced. Nevertheless, he did make it clear, like St. Paul before King Agrippa, calmly, reasonably, that he had committed no crime. "I speak the words of truth. . . ." He proclaimed his love of the Chinese people and his willingness to suffer, even to die, to show that love.

The two prisoners spent the night in the Kaying jail. And in the cell where Bishop Ford spent the night, his unjust judge—according to a Christian who later escaped to Hong Kong—one month later took his own life. Another Christian, who managed to reach the British colony, has given this bit of information: "In the hope of being able to see them for the last time, we rushed to the front door of the jail early next morning. We saw Bishop Ford and Sister Joan Marie, but we were not permitted to talk with them. We could only pray for them."

Still manacled with ropes, their arms held tight behind their backs, painfully pulling back their head and shoulders, they were led from the Kaying prison to the public bus stop where a waiting truck was to take them to Canton, the Kwangtung capital. Through the streets of the city he loved so dearly, the Bishop marched, bound now like a common, dangerous criminal, taunted, jeered, and reviled by the students who lined the streets. There was still proud dignity in his head held high.

This final ignominious walk through the streets of his See city was not without its comforting and consoling moments. The first refreshment came when his friend the Christian umbrella man and his family, standing by the roadside outside their shop, dropped to their knees and, with tears streaming down their faces, blessed themselves as the Bishop and Sister passed by. They were the good shepherd's glory and his joy. Farther along the road to the bus stop a Christian shoemaker, defying the new regime, broke from the angry mob and reached the Bishop to kiss his bound hands and ask for a blessing. They took courage from his courage. Seeing them so loyal, risking their lives to demonstrate their faith, helped to drown out the vicious shouts of "down with the imperialist," "death to the American spy." The incredible scene of organized hatred must have seemed more a dream than a reality, as though a devoted father were to hear his own children clamoring for his death. After thirty-three years of service in China, did he, in fact, hear his name shouted by the clenched-fisted mob, "Death to Ford, the spy!"?

An eyewitness to the scene, a Christian now living in Hong Kong, recalls how the Bishop and the nun boarded the truck for Canton. A small group of Christians had escorted the prisoners to the bus station, their hearts filled with sorrow and indignation. Many of the Catholics were weeping for they realized they would never see them again. "There was nothing we could do," he said, "but pray silently and beg God to protect them on their pitiful journey." The loyal Christian proudly said, "some of us remained at the bus station until the truck pulled out."

Ford took one last look at his beloved See city, and

he wept over it. To the end he would surely have remembered the agony of that parting. He had dreamed of Kaying becoming wholly Christian.

The first stop on the route from Kaying to Canton was the town of Hingning. Years before, when he was short of personnel, Ford had taken over the mission in this town as temporary pastor. He was well known to many of the non-Christian business men in Hingning as well as to his congregation. He returned in fetters; the honor of his episcopal elevation an additional personal humiliation.

A military escort had been alerted and was waiting for the prisoners at the bus terminal on the edge of town. It had been decided to parade the two America "spies" along the main street to the police headquarters to humiliate them. A wall of shouting, screaming middle school students lined the road armed with sticks and stones and refuse. Both prisoners were struck repeatedly by thrown objects; both were severely beaten. Sister Joan Marie recalls how one of the students thrust a stick between the Bishop's legs and tripped him. When he fell, the students began to club him as the guards looked on. The crowd, carried away with its madness, got completely out of hand. The guards moved away helplessly, and the two prisoners were left to the accumulated fury and the vicious frenzy of the youths. There was horrible, incredible confusion. The two missioners received blow after blow till their bodies were numb; they could scarcely move. Only the quiet, unshakable dignity of the Bishop saved their lives. Sister Joan Marie remembers that the Bishop fell three times to the rough dirt road; each time he picked himself up with great effort and calmly continued his *via dolorosa* through the mad mob. He looked neither right nor left; his eyes fixed straight ahead. Never did he try to defend himself or accuse those who treated him so shamefully.

194

The prisoners spent that night in the Hingning prison. The Bishop fell limp on the concrete floor unable to move. Sister Joan Marie, torn and battered from the long ordeal, bruised from the vicious beatings, was made to sit upon an improvised throne. Years later she could recollect feeling simple disgust that her habit was an unsightly mess from the refuse hurled at her on the nightmarish walk from the bus stop. Townspeople and students, brought in to pass before her, shouted taunts, Where is your God now? Where is the powerful American army now? and called her an imperialist spy.

After a sleepless night and a hasty breakfast of cold rice, the prisoners were bundled off early the next morning. At each town where the truck stopped, or where they were forced to remain in jail overnight, the routine was the same. At Lao Lung on the western edge of the Kaying Diocese another demonstration had been arranged, but a heavy rain cut down the crowd and spared them somewhat. Here Sister persuaded her guard, a young man from Hingning, to get some eggs and milk for the bishop. The food seemed to restore him, though he was still pitifully weak. They were then put aboard a small river boat for the trip to Waichow. The original ropes were exchanged at this point for heavier ones which were first soaked in water. As the rope dried, it tightened on their arms and shoulders pulling their heads back and inflicting excruciating pain.

At Waichow, they were removed from the boat and placed aboard a truck for Cheung Muk Tau. Here they were placed in the town prison to await the train that would take them to Canton. Sister Joan Marie recalls the experience here as the most abusive they had to endure on the long journey. Walking from the bus terminal to the prison, some students, in their white-hot mockery, tied a piece of heavy rope on the bishop's back. It hung from the base of his spine like a tail, much to the diabolical amusement of the crowd. Along the way youngsters carried signs describing the crimes of the two Americans and calling for their deaths. On the way to the Cheung Muk Tau prison they were halted several times for public questioning and accusations. When finally they reached the prison they were both searched, although it should have been obvious they possessed nothing. To further humiliate the Bishop and embarrass Sister, the prison guards forced the Bishop to remove all his clothing and remain naked during the questioning. After the senseless, repetitious interrogations, they were led off to cells for the night.

Canton Prison

They were four days enroute to Canton, four days which for them were but one monstrous night, four days during which only the omnipresent guards stood unchanging through the flux of dreams and waves of screaming students clamoring for their deaths. Several times along the way the Bishop had sunk into a swoon, broken by feverish dreams and groans. At last the journey came to an end. The prison wall seemed a haven after the days of nerve-wracking torture endured on the way. At the Canton prison gate, Ford had one of the rare unguarded moments when he was free to address a word of comfort to Sister Joan Marie. He whispered, "We're going to prison in honor of Christ and it is no disgrace."

Because of the crowded conditions in the large provincial prison, they were crammed into separate sections of an annex near the main building. Sister Joan Marie was shoved into a cell already occupied by seventeen women prisoners. There were no beds or cots in the prison; no towels, soap, toothbrushes, or wash basins. The prisoners slept on the cold, damp concrete floor.

Bishop Ford was too weak to work, but Sister Joan Marie was forced to join a women's work squad carrying water.

There were tedious hours of Communist indoctrination, brainwashing, and interminable questioning. Beginning early in the morning, these exhausting sessions would continue, with only short breaks for some rice and a brief rest, until several hours after dark. The two missioners were told to search their minds, to recall the various occasions on which they spoke out against Communism and against the new People's Government of China; to recall the number of times they had acted as spies for the imperialist American government. Their trial was repeated many times before different judges with the same old accusations, and the same old verdict.

After several weeks in the annex they were moved to the main section of the prison. Bishop Ford, according to an Austrialian fellow prisoner, William James, "was held in a small (ten by six foot) cell with three Chinese prisoners." After his release, James, in an August second, 1952, *New York Herald Tribune* article, said the Bishop was "berated often by the prison guards." The August 22nd, 1952, Hong Kong *Sunday Examiner* carried an interview with James in which he spoke of the khaki pants and shirt Bishop Ford was wearing and told of the prison diet of rice, cabbage, and water. James said he never spoke with the Bishop, but saw him occasionally through a crack in his cell door when the Bishop was brought out for questioning.

Occasionally, in their efforts to break the two Maryknollers, the accusers and indoctrinators would resort to physical violence. Sister Joan Marie wondered how the

197

Bishop could remain calm and controlled under this relentless attempt to make him admit guilt. He was ill and weary. The buoyant optimism had long since left him. He was approaching the late afternoon of his lifetime and he knew it. Vitality was ebbing, the ceaseless strain and throbbing pain must have been incredible. And there was no medication to dull his senses. Sister feared that "his lack of adequate food, his illness, and his generally weakened condition would make it impossible for him to continue." He had survived the oppressive humid heat of summer; she doubted that he could stand the cold dampness of a prison winter.

In this abyss of misery, the two missioners were deprived even the fellowship of mutual sufferers. The other prisoners, in order to obtain some extra food or a special favor, would spy on the Bishop or on the Sister and report fabricated offenses. Many well-to-do merchants and some Nationalist sympathizers obviously had succumbed to the brainwashing. They were seeking opportunities to prove they were loyal by bringing accusations against the two Americans. Suspicion, hate, and deceit filled the prison.

The two Maryknollers were never questioned together. Sister recalls how she caught a glimpse of the Bishop a few weeks after they entered the Canton prison. This was early in May 1951. A few months later, the guards brought the Bishop to the Sister's cell. The stumbling bag of bones, scarcely able to walk, was made to take off his clothes and stand in abject humiliation before her. She did not see him again until January 1952. This time she glimpsed him through a crack in the high gateway that separated the women's and the men's prison yards. Bishop Ford, she recalls, was sitting very close to the gate with his back to her. She said, "His neck was very thin and his hair was white. He was wearing a little woolen cap. His padded Chinese coat hung loosely on him . . . he was very thin." When the Bishop stood up, she remembers he reeled on his feet almost losing his balance. He extended both his arms in an effort to regain control over his body. The other prisoners laughed at his feeble attempts to move and told him to hurry, for the sentries had ordered them to withdraw from the yard.

Watching this scene in imagination years later, Sister could hear the guard order one of the other prisoners to hurry Ford along. The Bishop tottered a few steps, saying he could go no faster. The prisoner pulled the Bishop by the arm. He stumbled and fell helplessly to his knees. "I turned away in utter horror," she said, "for I could not stand the sight of him in such agony." When she again peeked through the gate she saw the other prisoner squatting down to let the Bishop throw his arms around his neck. And then he was dragged away. His chalice of suffering surely had filled to overflowing; it must have been hard for him to recognize himself. A character so strong, tormented by a body so weak.

"I didn't see his face during this time," she said, "but his legs hung loose like those of a ragdoll, so thin, so painfully limp. He seemed hardly to have strength enough to hold on to his helper who carried him without effort; the Bishop was not much more than a skeleton. The prison Simon of Cyrene made some remark to the sentries and they all laughed." He had come to the end he most dreaded, the slow dying he anticipated years before the Communists took over Kaying when he was talking about the Communist atrocities in the north: "When you say your prayers, pray that when it comes, it comes quickly. It is the long, drawn-out martyrdoms that are the hardest to take."

Two days later, Sister Joan Marie recalls how she

saw him again through the crack in the big gate. She had only a fleeting glimpse, for it was against the rule to peek into the other yard. "This time," she said, "I saw him plainly. His right arm was linked in the arm of another prisoner. In his left hand the Bishop held a cane to help support himself. Still, he was moving with great difficulty— little more than shuffling with tiny steps. I got a good look at his face, once so full and smiling, so strong and sure. Now he was emaciated, looking like an old man of a hundred years. His beard looked like white cotton, his hair was white and long. He seemed to be talking to the other prisoner. His face, as I saw it for the last time and remember it, was still calm and peaceful." Holding his fellow prisoner's arm, Sister saw him walking toward the sentries, who escorted his skeletal body back to the funereal chill of his cell as they had on the occasion two days before. She felt that the Bishop was "waiting on the beach"; the waters were rising, the waves would soon wash over him.

Sister Joan Marie was to get one final sight of Bishop Ford. It was a chilly day toward the end of January 1952. As the dark, dank atmosphere of the prison pierced through the marrow of her bones, the frail, emaciated nun in ragged Chinese garments limped along a gloomy corridor. On her shoulder she carried a coolie's bamboo pole from the ends of which dangled two five-gallon tins of water. Her bare feet suddenly went from under her and she slipped with a painful thud to the wet concrete floor. As she struggled to rise, she paused for breath. From her prone position she could see through the slits in the low ventilator of the wooden door. To her horror and amazement she saw her Bishop. "This time," she said, "he was being carried up the stairs from the lower end of the cell block. I know it was Bishop Ford, but I cannot describe his appearance. I was ill myself at the time and confused. He was not being carried on the prisoner's back as on previous occasions; this time he was slung over the shoulders of another prisoner and looked like a sack of potatoes." Life and laughter were gone; solitude and death were his only companions. This was the last time, as far as is known, that friendly eyes ever saw the Bishop of Kaying.

An Exile's Death

In April, the prison warden asked Sister if she knew what had happened to Bishop Ford's wristwatch. She replied that she did not know and added, "He is here in the prison, why don't you ask him?" There was no reply.

On August 16, 1952, Sister Joan Marie was called to the warden's office for more questioning. At the end of the session, she was told that Bishop Ford was dead. This was the first news she had had of his death six months before. According to the warden's statement, the Bishop succumbed on February twenty-first.

Shortly after Sister had been given the death notice, she was shown six photographs of the Bishop supposedly taken in a hospital. One showed his emaciated body in a bed with a doctor and nurse in attendance at his side. The Bishop's head was swathed in bandages with a small woolen cap on top. His face was clean shaven, but terribly thin. His eyes sunk deep in their sockets. The pictures were close-ups and showed a man dying, or possibly already dead. The guards refused to give Sister the pictures, although they promised to do so later on. She asked for some of the Bishop's personal effects but was refused. Sister signed a document attesting to the fact that "Francis Xavier Ford died on February 21, 1952, of a natural illness and old age, despite the expert medical care given him by the People's Government." The long lonely battle had come to an end just a month after Bishop Ford turned sixty years old.

Following the news, Sister Joan Marie herself fell gravely ill and the prison authorities transferred her to a hospital in Canton. On the first of September, after two weeks in the hospital, she was brought to an old potters' field in an isolated spot outside the city where she was shown the Bishop's grave. On a rough granite slab about three feet high were engraved the three Chinese characters which were the phonetic reproduction of his name in Mandarin, FU ER TET (FORD). Under his name was the word for grave. The day, month, and year of his death were written on the side of the marker. She recalls that the paint on the slab was still wet when she knelt beside the grave. Undoubtedly, the markings had been prepared for her visit. She thought of the Bishop's hasty burial in the bitter dampness of that day in February: no pageantry, no solemn requiem, no sorrowful mourners, no tolling of bells. No Chinese newspaper carried a notice of his death. But she knew, too, that that was the way her Bishop would have preferred it: he had never liked funerals anyhow.

Many Christians later visited the grave and prayed there; bits of weeds and grass were picked up and carried away as mementoes. This went on for several years. Later, however, refugees coming from the Canton area brought word to Hong Kong that the cemetery had been converted into a rice field. All the grave markers had been destroyed. There is now no trace of the place where the hungry earth, "with neither grief nor malice," received the burden of Francis Xavier Ford's bones. In the years to come there will be many layers of dust and there will be many rains upon that dust. The seed has died and there will be life for the Bishop's people.

A few days after her visit to the Bishop's grave, Sister Joan Marie was ordered out of the country as an undesirable alien who had betrayed the people of China. Ford's death made it no longer necessary to have her around as a witness at the final trial they had planned for him. On September eleventh she was expelled. After the train ride from Canton to the border town of Sum Chun she was escorted to the bridge leading into the British Crown Colony of Hong Kong. Weeping from exhaustion and privation, she stumbled across the bridge to freedom. She was taken to the Maryknoll Sisters' Convent School in Kowloon where she gave to the world the news of Bishop Ford's death—seven months after he had died.

Foreigners—Out!

Sister Joan Marie was not the first missioner to cross the Sum Chun Bridge. The Red rulers gradually gained their objective of driving all foreigners from the country. The bamboo curtain was slowly lowered and the death knell of apostolic work in China was sounded. Hundreds of missioners of all nationalities and all denominations made their way from their adopted land into the free air of the British Crown Colony, some so weakened in body and mind that they slumped unconscious to the ground on realizing that they were free. Each had his own sad story of ruthless treatment, each carried his own marks of violent abuse, each expressed his sorrow at leaving behind his life's work and his Christians who were now as sheep without a shepherd. Some retained the look of fear for weeks; some few never did regain complete peace of mind.

In Kaying after Ford's arrest all mission buildings were occupied by Communist officials. The Christians were summoned several times to the magistracy where Communist officials harangued them about the crimes of the American missioners and the United States government. The image of America as the young revolutionary country whose historic example had influenced Sun Yat-sen had long since vanished: America was no longer the model for people seeking to shake off colonialism, striving to embark upon their own destiny free of outside influence and control; no longer the promoter and encourager of change, no longer the dream of the common man. Americans were now the despised enemy—the sole foe, embodying all the evils of the hated West. In the Communists' *Current Affairs Handbook* there is a chapter entitled: *How To Hold An Accusation Meeting*. "All accusations," is says, "must be directed against U.S. imperialism, the implacable enemy of the Chinese people."

Chinese priests, too, were rounded up by the Communist police and accused of unimaginable crimes against the People's Government. A fierce campaign of hate and lies was set in motion and the incredible became credible. So often were the accusations against the missioners repeated, so outrageous were the indignant tones of the angry accusers, that people who had been friendly to the missioners—even some otherwise loyal Christians—reluctantly admitted that the crimes must be real. Some Chinese Christians reasoned this way: the doctrine of the Church was still true, but perhaps some of its leaders were indeed agents of imperialist America, spies who were using religion as a front to deceive the Chinese people. Some of these people were found taking an active part in the so-called treason trials shouting "away with the foreigners!"

A short time after the Communists took over, a missioner in Hong Kong received a note from one of Kaying's former catechists: "Since the 'liberation' of China," he wrote, "the church and the religious schools have been either closed or taken over by the government. All mission activities are prohibited, even Sunday Mass is disallowed. They consider that the Church is the aggressive bureau of American imperialism and the missioners are its spies. We Catholics are regarded as assistants of this imperialism. That is why some have been imprisoned and others are suspect. No one dares to visit another. Everyone is in danger."

As the Communists turned their attention to the Church in China, they tried to alienate its members from all foreign influence. They set up a Chinese Catholic Church entirely independent of Rome. To accomplish this, the new government placed all the Chinese Fathers in custody. Some were sent to Swatow, others to Canton for questioning and indoctrination. All of the Kaying Chinese priests refused to cooperate in the formation of the new schismatic church. Some were incarcerated for short-term prison sentences on charges of cooperating with the imperialist spy, Ford. Father Paul Lam was seen in chains in the Kaying prison. The native Sisters had already returned to their respective villages as Ford had told them to. They were able to support themselves by sewing and cooking. Courageously they helped the Christian community, encouraging them, consoling them and on occasion bringing the Blessed Sacrament to those who were dying. But the prospects for the Church in Kaying in the 1950's were far from bright.

Father Aloysius Au briefly described these conditions in a note that he was able to send to a friend in Hong Kong. "Conditions have not improved," he said; "Holy Mass and the Sacraments are taboo, but I say Mass without vestments or lights. . . . Most of the Christians are afraid to come for Mass. . . . Believe me, when I got out of jail I had almost forgotten how to celebrate Mass. Mass prayers and liturgy seemed so strange. . . ."

By 1954, word from a Kaying Chinese priest received in Hong Kong stated that the "influence of the Church in Kaying seems to have almost disappeared. The Catholics do not dare let themselves be heard for fear of trouble. The Reds have countless ways and means of detection. It is their aim to drive Christianity out of the region." And so the Church, for the time being, will cease to grow in China because she ceases to be free.

The Kaying priest's report went on to explain that the old Christians might remain faithful to their religious beliefs, but in the homes of Christians there were to be no signs of the "Western" religion, no holy pictures, no crucifix on the wall. One old Christian man was ordered by the authorities to remove a picture of Christ from the walls of his house. In the face of abuse and threats he refused and remained adamant. The Communists surprisingly yielded. In disgust they said as they left: "Well, he is an old man and of no use to the cause anyway."

In 1958, the Communists called a Provincial Conference of eighty Chinese priests and about forty Catholic lay leaders in Canton. Among them were eight priests and three lay leaders from Kaying. The theme of the meeting was the necessity of severing all ties with the foreign or universal Church. During this conference, two Kaying priests about whom there had been doubt, spoke out before the assembly against Maryknoll and against Bishop Ford. "In the future," one of them shouted, "I shall have nothing to do with the Vatican or with the Maryknoll missioners. I shall refuse to receive money . . . from the American imperialist acting through the Maryknoll missioners, because these are the enemies of the Chinese people."

Then this defecting priest was joined by another from Kaying denouncing in a slanderous manner Bishop Ford and many of the Maryknoll priests who had been in Kaying. Several times during the conference, the two unfortunate priests accused the "so-called missioners" of coming to China not to save souls, but to engage in espionage, "to enslave the Chinese people with their imperialistic doctrine."

This would have been the hardest of all blows for Bishop Ford if he had heard one of his beloved Chinese priests accuse him of disloyalty to China. He could overlook the hatred of his hostel students and the indifference of some of his Christians, but the Chinese priests were his pride and his consolation, his hope for the future.

In a note smuggled into Hong Kong sometime during 1958, Father Au gives this picture of his life in Red China: "Every day I walk to a market place about six miles away, to carry firewood, coal or beans. I am able now to balance about one hundred pounds with a pole on my shoulders and I make about fifty cents in local currency for each trip. Not much . . . and it is very hard . . . but the toil and effort are far outbalanced by the spiritual gain, for I am offering my suffering for the salvation of souls. . . . I am suffering from hemorrhoids and my teeth are giving me a lot of trouble. The authorities continually ask me about the Legion of Mary. Please say a prayer for me now and then. . . ."

Sometime later, a brief, still more disheartening word reached Hong Kong in Father Au's handwriting saying, "I shall hang on as long as I possibly can; I cannot leave my flock. I feel so oppressed; I am really physically sick." And again a few months later, "Be assured that we'll be faithful to Christ and would rather choose death than do anything that would cause another sword to pierce His Sacred Heart. . . . There is no sign of easing off . . . it seems they are determined to squash the Church. Being a former pastor and member of the diocesan council, I am always the butt of their endless probing and indignities. I am mentioning this not to indulge in self-pity . . . but I feel you should know the facts and the conditions at this end."

Father Au asked his friend in Hong Kong to notify his family in Penang if he should be put to death. "The clouds are gathering again," he wrote, "and I am afraid of the impending storm. . . . We really need much prayer." During the mouth of February 1960, Father Au was again arrested and accused of refusing to cooperate with the new Chinese Catholic Church. This time his place of incarceration was in the far-distant province of Chinghai, near the Tibet-Sinkiang border, where only hardened criminals and unrepentant enemies of the Communist regime were sent. The following year word reached Hong Kong that the noble, courageous priest had died in Chinghai's "Reform-by-Labor" prison on November 23, 1960.

Another Chinese priest, still alive, still faithful, wrote the following note to a friend in Hong Kong: "I was sentenced to twelve years of prison [and] . . . they sent me to a Labor Camp. Over ten thousand prisoners are working here. We dig coal. It is very difficult work, we must work ten hours a day, every day. The food is very little. Twice a day some rice and vegetables . . . my health is very poor. I may break down altogether soon. . . "

There is little doubt that the Communist authorities know the whereabouts of the Chinese priests who remained in the Kaying diocese after Bishop Ford was arrested in April 1951. Scraps of news from time to time have been brought out to Hong Kong by Christian refugees. All of the loyal priests have suffered greatly for their faith, inside and outside of prison. Some were able during their time in prison to preach and even to baptize. One young priest, released after five years in prison, returned to his native village and was seen in tears early the next morning kneeling on the steps of the village church. He could not enter the building because it had been locked and boarded up by the liberation authorities. How proud Bishop Ford would have been of his faithful Chinese priests. It was all there: the struggle between good and evil, missionary zeal, persecution, the refusal to compromise. One day the glorious story of Bishop Ford's Kaying Chinese priests will be told. It will be, with only a few exceptions, a story of loyalty and courage seldom met in the history of the Church.

There is no evidence that the mainland Chinese leaders have changed their minds about Christianity. A Communist policy article in the *Peking Review* of March 1966 makes this very clear. Entitled *Hyprocrisy of Missionary Activities*, it said in part: "In the past, in the name of philanthropy, American missionaries have run schools and hospitals in the hinterlands . . . in order to poison the minds of the local people. They also used this means to gather local information and carry out subversion in co-ordination with the political, economic and military needs of the U.S. government. But now the mounting struggle for liberation. . . . has compelled U.S. imperialism to modify its tactics and adopt more hypocritical and covert methods in its missionary activities overseas. . . . Churches are deliberately given an indigenous character and religious rites a national form. Local churchmen are encouraged to take the limelight while American missionaries act behind the scenes. . . . These missionaries also use modern means of communication to put across imperialist ideas and the 'American way of life.' "

In the eyes of the Communists of China, Christ is a symbol of the West, just as for Westerners Buddha is a symbol of the East. The vast majority of Chinese do not know Christ, nor do they understand the Christian doctrine of love. They know only the grasping, colonial West and what it had done to them through the years.

EPILOGUE

"Is he one who is appointed to an exile's death? Yes, by all means. Is that a cause for sorrow? Not at all."

These prophetic words were spoken by Maryknoll's Father James M. Drought in his sermon at the consecration ceremony of his friend Bishop Francis Xavier Ford on September 21, 1935. An exile's death was not a cause for sorrow because, in Father Drought's words, "before death shall come, he will preach the Gospel to the poor in spirit. . . . He will explain to their incredulous astonishment the transforming power of the Beatitudes . . . he will call forth the meek, the mournful and the clean of heart. He brings not the framework of civilization, but charity which is its soul. Is it enough then to preach Christ? Yes, enough today as long ago when Peter preached and Paul. Many may not heed . . . and so the apostle may pass by with few to note his passing."

The "exile's death" to which Father Drought then so eloquently referred was the missioner's separation from his home—Ford's separation from his family and home, from his American friends and relatives. But Francis X. Ford had long ago died to all of these. From the moment he had reached China in 1918, his home had been wherever his Chinese mission was; his relatives and friends were his Chinese converts and his Chinese neighbors.

On February 21, 1952, in a Communist prison cell in Canton, Francis X. Ford did indeed die an exile's death—exiled from his Chinese mission and from his Chinese Christians whom he so dearly loved. Of his death Bishop Fulton Sheen had this to say: "There is only one thing we do know, and that is that the blood of this great Maryknoller, of this great American, of this first American bishop to be martyred in China is to be counted among some of the noblest blood that this earth has drunk since Calvary drank the blood of Christ."

Maryknollers throughout the world were saddened when they received word of Bishop Ford's death; but they were proud of the courageous manner in which the pioneer member of the Society worked and suffered for his people. There was no fanfare, no rush to enroll him in the catalogue of the saints or martyrs, but there was a strong feeling that the Bishop had given his life for the faith. No missioner could give more than that. However, many Maryknollers were puzzled by the fact that there was no bold demand by our State Department for an explanation from Red China —no righteous indictment handed up to the bar of public opinion. A few strong voices in America, however, did express sincere indignation.

Hearst columnist, Bob Considine, in his September 12, 1952, syndicated column, was moved to write: "The next time you feel on the verge of self-pity because of some real or imagined example of ingratitude shown you, try to remember a man from Brooklyn named Francis Xavier Ford. Ford loved the Chinese people who in the end put him to death. He was a man passionately devoted to the underdog . . . he gave his all to them. . . ." The *New York Times* on September 12 bitterly reported: "We know by now what to expect of Mao Tse-tung's ruffians. . . . The murderers of Bishop Ford . . . have no claim upon our sympathy. They have put themselves beyond the pale." Father Gillis, the famous Paulist missioner remarked that Ford "did not die for colonialism or capitalism, he died for the faith. We should not sing a sad Requiem, but a triumphant Te Deum." When Ford's close friend Bishop Philip Furlong heard the news he said: "We are saddened by the thought that the Church has lost his great mind . . . we are pleased by the thought that we have known and lived so close to a Christian martyr." Bishop Fulton J. Sheen had lost a friend also; with deep feeling he wrote: "We plead with all American Catholics, with all mission societies, to beg the Church to study his life and to tell us if we may venerate him. . . ."

A memorial Mass for Bishop Ford was celebrated with great solemnity in the Hong Kong Cathedral on September 14, the Feast of the Exaltation of the Holy Cross. The striking symbolism in the liturgy of that day was appropriately significant as a memorial service for a dead missioner. Archbishop Anthony Riberi, the Apostolic Delegate to China, delivered the eulogy. "Today," he said, "there is a temptation to gloom and despair among those of us who are weak in faith as we see the sturdy oaks of the Christian Church, such as Bishop Ford, being cut down, and the cross that was planted with such great labor and pain, uprooted by a grim and relentless foe of God and religion. Let us have courage and confidence in the One who said: 'fear not, I am with you all days. . . .' Bishop Ford's death is not in vain. Thanks to his inspiring example, the soil of China will sprout with crosses that will make it the fairest field of Christendom. Have we not the assurance of Christ Himself? 'Unless the grain of wheat fall into the ground and die, it remains alone. But if it die, it brings forth much fruit.' " That is the mysterious law of our living.

To keep his memory green, memorials have sprung up in many cities: the Bishop Ford Center in Hong Kong; the Bishop Ford Boy's High School in Brooklyn; St. Luke's Bishop Ford parish hall in Dayton, and the Bishop Ford Student Center in Taiwan built and directed by the former Kaying priest, Father Mark Chai.

The mission life of Francis Xavier Ford was another experience in the Church's long history. During his more than three decades of missionary service he was foremost in many apostolic endeavors. He realized the necessity for a Chinese secular clergy when many bishops in China were hesitant about the fitness of Chinese young men for the priesthood. He understood the role of Brothers and lay-men in mission work when many missioners thought that priests alone should direct the activities of the Church. He pioneered the participation of missionary Sisters in the direct apostolate when most missionary Sisters were engaged exclusively in institutional works of charity. He founded a community of Chinese Sisters to spread the gospel message when it was rare in the interior of China for women to visit the homes of strangers or to act as teachers of religion. He adapted features of Chinese architecture when most missioners were content with a slavish copy of Western churches and buildings.

From the surface to whatever depths one may care to examine his life, each layer rings true. Whatever defects there may have been were trivialities. It does not matter much that his knowledge of the language was inadequate, that some of his programs did not succeed, or that he occasionally lost patience with lesser brains.

What does matter much is that his thirty-four years in China have enriched the experience of those everywhere who dedicate their lives to the service of others. He was peculiarly and indigenously American, yet he made every effort to become Chinese. Beyond Kaying and Maryknoll he may never become a legend, but for those who knew him, he will be the embodiment of something forever noble and true.

As to the immediate fruit of his sacrifice we can but dimly conjecture. The time and manner of harvesting that fruit is uncertain. However, this uncertainty in no way undoes the conviction of the hope itself. Bishop Ford is part of mankind's unfailing expectation.

PRAYER

Lord Jesus, give to all of us to know the urgent need of saving souls. Give to our hearts the light of Thy Spirit to see the priceless souls that must be saved; to find the means to obtain their speedy ransom, and the strengthened will to spend ourselves in the service of Thy heathen sons. Amen.

POEM

I saw Him peeping at the dawn, His smile in waving grass and fern, His whisper in the stir of wings. In storm and wind His power. Searching for God who hid Himself.

> Then one day in a Chinese town
> I saw a man and caught
> A fleeting glimpse of Him long lost
> Whom once I vainly sought
> Again and yet again; and now
> In every man I meet
> He is revealed—but changed in face
> No longer smiling sweet.
> I cried, "Forgive them for they know
> Thee not nor what they do."
> He answered eagerly, " 'Tis yours
> To pardon them, and you
> Can quench My thirst, baptizing them,
> Anointing with My oil
> These least of brethren, bruised by sin;
> 'Tis then for Me you toil."

The vigil lights of heaven nod and sleep
When massing taper from the East is borne
    And Earth's great Sacrifice begun
    Of God's anointed, Mary's Son;
The Dayspring from On High a tryst will keep
Dispelling night at the approach of Dawn.

FRANCIS XAVIER FORD

INDEX

219